ON CENSORSHIP

(Above) The Romani Goya: T Goulden
(Cover) Ray Hamilton: Camera Press

INDEX ON CENSORSHIP 3 1994

Index on Censorship (ISSN 0306-4220) is published
bimonthly by a non-profit-making company: Writers
& Scholars International Ltd, Lancaster House,
33 Islington High Street, London N1 9LH
Phone: 071-278 2313
Fax: 071-278 1878

Index on Censorship is associated with Writers &
Scholars Educational Trust, registered charity
number 325003

Second class postage (US subscribers only) paid at
Irvington, New Jersey. Postmaster: send US address
changes to Index on Censorship c/o Virgin Mailing
& Distribution, 10 Camptown Road, Irvington, NJ
07111

Subscriptions 1994 (6 issues p.a.): £30 (overseas
£36 or US$48). Students £23/US$35

© This selection Writers & Scholars International Ltd,
London 1994

© Contributors to this issue, except where
otherwise indicated

Printed in UK by Unwin Brothers Limited

Former Editors: Michael Scammell (1972-81); Hugh Lunghi (1981-83); George Theiner (1983-88); Sally Laird (1988-89); Andrew Graham-Yooll (1989-93)

EDITORIAL

Trade, aid and human rights

It may have been something of a facade, but facades have their uses. The human rights conditions imposed by the US Congress on military aid and trade privileges — linkage, as it's come to be called — offered endless loopholes and many and various ingenious opportunities for evasion. But the statement did, as Bob Sutcliffe says in another context, that of immigration, help to define 'some shared concept of what is desirable and acceptable.' At the end of May, renewing China's Most Favoured Nation status for a further year, Bill Clinton announced he was breaking the link between the status and human rights, finally demolishing even the facade. Not long afterwards, Douglas Hurd, the British Foreign Secretary, described as 'naive' the notion that trade and human rights can be linked.

Democratic leaders in Congress have since broken with Clinton's policy by introducing a bill to re-establish the linkage. Silvino Berlusconi, hardly the protagonist of liberal values, has recently met the Dalai Lama in the face of Chinese government protests, and has begun to speak a different language on international human rights. There are plenty of cynical explanations for this, of course — but then what could be more cynical, as Noam Chomsky recounts, than the US insistence in Vienna last summer that it would oppose any attempt to use religious and cultural traditions to weaken the concept of universal human rights, and yet to make so many compromises over these rights in the name of that holy of holies, trade.

Trade, a critical aspect of those 'vital interests' that led the West to intervene massively in oil-rich Kuwait but to wash its hands sanctimoniously of under-endowed Bosnia and Rwanda, is fast becoming the only criterion for action. As in the days of empire, the gunboats are there to fight trade wars; genocide, the ultimate violation of human rights, we merely deplore.

In this second issue of the new *Index* we also examine the daily and increasing violation of the rights of Europe's migrants. Now as much as 25 per cent of the population, migrants are frequently denied any voice or representation within the present structure of recognised human rights. Increasingly, the 'good' migrant is one who is fleeing political persecution, a 'bad' migrant is simply looking for a materially better life. In practice, the right to cross arbitrary borders depends, once again, on the 'interest' of the receiving — or rejecting — state: the inexorable and absurd logic of the market increasingly measures only the profit that accrues from this trade in humanity.

Ursula Owen

CONTENTS

Volume 23 (New Series) No 3 July/August 1994   158   ISSN 0306 4220

Volume 23 (New Series) No 3 July/August 1994   158   ISSN 0306 4220

LETTERS

TV violence
Will the real villain please stand up

From Gara LaMarche
*Associate Director of
Human Rights Watch and
Director of its Free Expression Project*

Anne Nelson's essay in the May/June 1994 *Index* [Colours of violence] reminds us that, often, violence is to the left as sex is to the right: a bugaboo that provides the occasion for muddled thinking and erosion of principle.

I am with Nelson when she starts out on this dangerous journey. America is a frighteningly violent society. This is no invention of ratings-hungry producers of local television news programmes or 'tabloid' shows. Poverty, racism and social disintegration have frayed the bonds of civilisation to the point where many inner-city neighbourhoods are like armed camps. The insane proliferation of guns and the laxity of their regulation provides a daily parade of shootings by disgruntled postal workers, abusive husbands, and pampered young lords of Beverley Hills.

I do not view all this from a position high above the battle: a suspected drug dealer was shot dead by undercover cops not 10 feet from my front door one recent afternoon; a local pizza parlour catering to families with children was invaded early one pre-Christmas evening by gun-toting robbers who pistol-whipped the owner and fired shots into the air, scattering terrified kids and parents under the tables.

Progressives like me — and Anne Nelson — have plenty of reason to be concerned about violence in our midst. I understand the frustration that causes many otherwise-sensible people to blame bottom-line obsessed television networks and Hollywood studios, always fair game for bashing. But I am mystified at the diversion of energies that has gone into this campaign, and troubled by the too-ready embrace of arguments and remedies that will come back to haunt free speech advocates.

Janet Reno, the US Attorney General who is threatening the television networks with government regulation if they don't 'voluntarily' clean up their act, should be using her bully pulpit to lead the fight for serious gun control. And what about other kinds of violence by agents of the state, from frequent police beatings of minority crime suspects (most often, away from the eye of a video camera) to the routinisation of executions? I know Anne Nelson cares about all these things, too. But I hope she is as bothered as I am by the weakness of a strong progressive counterweight to the (overlapping) gun, police and execution lobbies.

As for Nelson's arguments and remedies, it's a little hard to tell precisely what kind of regulation of media violence she would like to see, but she advances some upsetting notions in groping toward them. Commercial broadcasters of violent programming, she says, 'should be held responsible for the harmful effects of their product.' So, to use her own example, the makers of *The Deer Hunter* — by any measure, a serious, if graphic, drama about the horrors of war — could be sued by the survivors of the young men who imitated the Russian roulette scene.

The 'overwhelming' studies Nelson cites are in sharp dispute, but let's look at a few. Hitting and nail biting went up among Canadian children after the advent of television in the 1950s, while murder rates rose at the same time in the United States? The programming of that time was pacific by 1994 standards, and wouldn't be touched by even the most ardent of today's would-be violence regulators. Is Nelson claiming that television itself is the culprit?

I don't find it comforting that, in looking for precedents to justify government regulation of media violence, Nelson points to the regulation of pornography, with apparent approval of prosecutions against 'photographs of fully-clothed juveniles'. Just as I don't trust government censors to make a distinction between sex education material and 'hardcore' pornography, I don't trust them to sort out *Schindler's List* from *Nightmare on Elm Street*, or whatever it is Nelson would like to curb.

Creators, even tasteless and mercenary ones, must remain free. Condemn pointless violence, by all means, and work for a safer world. But keep the government out of the business of regulating speech and images.

NOAM CHOMSKY

Sweet home of liberty

A tale of justice
denied, rights
violated and
darkness at the
heart of the
enlightenment

(Left) Black Liberty: Panorama/Camera Press

In his preface to *Animal Farm*, George Orwell turned his attention to societies that are relatively free from state controls. 'The sinister fact about literary censorship in England,' he wrote, 'is that it is largely voluntary. Unpopular ideas can be silenced, and inconvenient facts kept dark, without any need for any official ban.' The outcome is in part ensured by control of the press by 'wealthy men who have every motive to be dishonest on certain important topics,' but more significantly, by the 'general tacit agreement that 'it wouldn't do' to mention that particular fact.' As a result, 'Anyone who challenges the prevailing orthodoxy finds himself silenced with surprising effectiveness.' The preface was published 30 years after the book appeared.

New York: shopping on Fifth Avenue

DMITRI KASTERINE/CAMERA PRESS

In the case under discussion here, the 'prevailing orthodoxy' is well summarised by historian Michael Howard: 'For 200 years the United States has preserved almost unsullied the original ideals of the Enlightenment..., and, above all, the universality of these values,' though unfortunately it 'does not enjoy the place in the world that it should have earned through its achievements, its generosity, and its goodwill since World War II' — indeed, 'for 200 years.' The record is unsullied by the treatment of 'that hapless race of native Americans, which we are exterminating with such merciless and perfidious cruelty' (John Quincy Adams) and the slaves who provided cheap cotton to allow the industrial revolution to take off 'through market forces'; by the fact that US aid 'has tended to flow disproportionately to Latin American governments which torture their citizens... to the hemisphere's relatively egregious violators of fundamental human rights' (Lars Schoultz, the leading academic specialist on human rights in Latin America); by the terrible atrocities the US was once again conducting in its 'backyard' as the praises were delivered; or by the fate of Filipinos, Vietnamese, and a few who might have a different story to tell.

A natural starting point for an inquiry into Washington's defence of 'the universality of [Enlightenment] values' is the Universal Declaration of Human Rights [UD] adopted by the UN General Assembly on 10 December 1948, accepted generally as a human rights standard and, in US courts, as 'customary international law'. The UD became the focus of great attention in June 1993, during the international conference on human rights in Vienna. A lead headline in the *New York Times* read: 'At Vienna Talks, US Insists Rights Must be Universal'. Washington warned 'that it would oppose any attempt to use religious and cultural traditions to weaken the concept of universal human rights', the *Times* reported. Secretary of State Warren Christopher declared that 'the United States will never join those who would undermine the Universal Declaration', and will defend their universality against those who hold 'that human rights should be interpreted differently in regions with non-Western cultures,' notably the 'dirty dozen', with Indonesia their advocate.

Washington's decisiveness prevailed. The 'challenge of relativity' was beaten back, the *New York Times* reported. The conference declared that 'the universal nature of these rights and freedoms is beyond question'; there will be no 'retreat from the basic tenets' of the UD.

The impressive rhetoric was rarely besmirched by inquiry into the observance of the UD by its defenders or even its actual provisions. These matters were raised in Vienna in a Public Hearing, held to break through the wall of silence erected to protect Western power from 'inconvenient facts'. Citizens of the free world are fortunate to have readily available to them the concerns of the vast majority of the world's people, in the report of the Public Hearing, *Justice Denied!*, published in an edition of 2,000 copies in Kathmandu.

Some of the provisions of the UD are familiar in the United States. The most famous by far is Article 13 (2), which states that 'Everyone has the right to leave any country, including his own'. Article 13 was invoked with much passion every year on Human Rights Day, 10 December, with public demonstrations and indignant demands that the Soviet Union let Russian Jews leave. To be exact, the words just quoted were invoked, but not the phrase that follows: 'and to return to his country'. The significance of the omitted words was spelled out on 11 December 1948, the day after the UD was ratified, when the General Assembly passed Resolution 194, which affirms the right of Palestinians to return to their homes or receive compensation, if they chose not to return. But it was always understood that it 'wouldn't do' to mention the omitted words, let alone the glaringly obvious fact that the most passionate opponents of Article 13 were the people exhorting the Soviet tyrants to observe it, to much acclaim.

It is only fair to add that the cynicism has now been overcome. At the December 1993 UN session, the Clinton administration for the first time joined with Israel in opposing UN 194, which was reaffirmed by a vote of 127-2. As is the norm, there was no report or comment. But at least the inconsistency is behind us: the first half of Article 13 (2) has lost its relevance, and Washington now officially rejects its second half.

Let us move on to Article 14, which affirms that 'Everyone has the right to seek and to enjoy in other countries asylum from persecution.' Haitians, for example, including the 87 new victims captured in Clinton's blockade and returned to their charnel house as the Vienna conference opened. The US has upheld Article 14 in this manner since the 1970s, the Duvalier dictatorship being a respected ally helping to convert Haiti to an export platform for US corporations seeking super-cheap labour. The practice was ratified in a Reagan-Duvalier agreement. When a military coup overthrew Haiti's first democratically elected president in September 1991, renewing the terror, the Bush administration imposed a blockade to drive back the flood of refugees to the torture chamber where they were to be imprisoned.

Bush's 'appalling' refugee policy was bitterly condemned by candidate Bill Clinton, whose first act as President was to tighten the illegal blockade while extending Bush's decision to exempt US firms from the OAS embargo. Trade with Haiti in violation of the embargo remained high in 1992 and increased by almost half under Clinton, including purchases by the US government and a large increase in export of food from the starving island. These are among the many devices adopted to ensure that the popular forces that swept President Aristide to power will have no voice in any future 'democracy,' no surprise to people who have failed to immunise themselves from 'inconvenient facts'.

Again, fairness requires that we recognise that Washington did briefly depart from this systematic rejection of Article 14. During the seven months of democracy, Washington gained a sudden and short-lived sensitivity to Article 14 as the flow of refugees declined to a trickle — in fact, reversed, as Haitians returned to their country in its moment of hope. Of the more than 24,000 Haitians intercepted by US forces from 1981 to 1991, 11 were granted asylum as victims of political persecution (in comparison with 75,000 out of 75,000 Cubans). In these years of terror, Washington allowed 28 asylum claims. During Aristide's tenure, with violence and repression radically reduced, 20 were allowed from a refugee pool perhaps 1/50th the scale. Practice returned to normal after the military coup and the renewed terror.

Concerned that popular pressures might make it difficult to sustain the blockade, the administration has been pleading with other countries to relieve the US of the burden of accommodating refugees. Curiously, debate over this issue has missed the obvious candidate: Tanzania, which

ROGER HUTCHINGS/CAMERA PRESS

Haiti: returned to the charnel house

has been able to accommodate hundreds of thousands of Rwandans, and could surely come to the rescue of the beleaguered USA by accepting a few thousand more black faces.

Article 25 of the UD states that 'Everyone has the right to a standard of living adequate for the health and well-being of himself and his family, including food, clothing, housing and medical care and necessary social services, and the right to security in the event of unemployment, sickness, disability, widowhood, old age or other lack of livelihood in circumstances beyond his control.' It is unnecessary to dwell on the defence of these principles in the world's richest country, with unparalleled advantages — and a poverty level twice that of England, which has the second worst record among the industrial societies. In the USA, 30 million people suffer from hunger, an increase of 50% since 1985; 40% of children in the world's richest city fall below the poverty line, deprived of minimal conditions that offer some hope of escape from misery, destitution, and violence; and on, and on.

Given its extraordinary advantages, the USA is in the leading ranks of opposition to the universality of the UD by virtue of this Article alone, with Britain not far behind.

Article 23 declares that 'Everyone has the right to work, to free choice of employment, to just and favourable conditions of work and to protection against unemployment,' along with 'remuneration ensuring for himself and his family an existence worthy of human dignity, and supplemented, if necessary, by other means of social protection.' Again, we need not tarry on the devotion to this principle. Furthermore, 'Everyone has the right to form and to join trade unions for the protection of his interests.'

The latter right is technically observed in the USA, though it is efficiently undermined by an array of legal and administrative mechanisms. Reviewing some of the methods, *Business Week* reports that 'Over the past dozen years, in fact, US industry has conducted one of the most successful anti-union wars ever, illegally firing thousands of workers for exercising their rights to organise. Unlawful firings occurred in one-third of all representation elections in the late '80s, versus 8 per cent in the late '60s.' Workers have no recourse, as the Reaganites converted the increasingly powerful state they nurtured to an expansive welfare state for the rich, defying US law as well as the customary international law enshrined in the Universal Declaration.

Under popular pressures rooted in the ferment of the 1960s, the US Congress has imposed human rights conditions on military aid and trade privileges. These actions have compelled the White House to find various modes of evasion, which became farcical during the Reagan years. The contortions on China are a recent example, though it is worth noting that many critical issues were not even raised: crucially, the horrifying conditions that 'free labour' is forced to endure, with hundreds of workers, mostly women, burned to death locked into factories, some 15,000 deaths from industrial accidents in 1993, and other gross violations of international conventions.

30 million people in the US suffer from hunger; 40% of children fall below the poverty line in the world's richest city

The role of sanctions is well illustrated by the case of the voice of the 'dirty dozen,' Indonesia. Its horrendous human rights record at home and near-genocidal aggression in East Timor has not led to sanctions, though Congress did cut off aid for military training in reaction to the Dili massacre. The aftermath followed the familiar pattern: delicately selecting the anniversary of the Indonesian invasion, Clinton's State Department announced that 'Congress's action did not ban Indonesia's purchase of training with its own funds', so it can proceed despite the ban. Rather than impose sanctions, or even limit military aid, the USA, UK, and other powers have sought to enrich themselves as much as possible by participating in Indonesia's crimes.

World leaders do recognise some limits, however. In November 1993, on behalf of the non-aligned movement and the World Health Organisation, Indonesia submitted to the UN a resolution requesting an opinion from the World Court on the legality of the use of nuclear weapons. In the face of this atrocity, the guardians of international morality leaped into action. The USA, UK, and France threatened Indonesia with trade sanctions and termination of aid, the Catholic Church press reported, unless it withdrew the resolution, as it did.

Meanwhile, terror and aggression continue unhampered, along with harsh repression of labour in a country with wages half those of China. The administration suspended review of Indonesian labour practices, commending Indonesia for 'bringing its labour law and practice into closer conformity with international standards' (Trade Representative Mickey Kantor), a witticism that is in particularly poor taste.

As the most powerful state, the USA makes its own laws, using force and conducting economic warfare at will. It also threatens sanctions against countries that do not abide by its conveniently

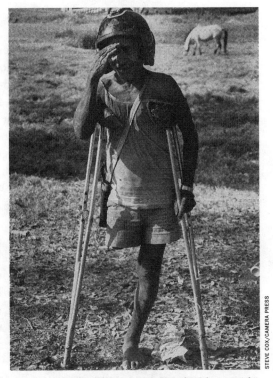

East Timor: a victim of US human rights

flexible notions of 'free trade.' Recently Washington has employed such threats with great effectiveness (and GATT approval) to force open Asian markets for US tobacco exports and advertising, aimed primarily at the growing markets of women and children. The US Agriculture Department also gives grants to tobacco firms to promote smoking overseas. Asian countries have attempted anti-smoking campaigns, but they are overwhelmed by the miracles of the market, reinforced by US power through the sanctions threat. Oxford University epidemiologist Richard Peto estimates that among Chinese children under 20 today, 50 million will die of cigarette-related diseases, an achievement that ranks high even by 20th century standards.

While state power energetically promotes the most lethal known form of substance abuse in the interests of agribusiness, it adopts highly selective devices in other cases. On the pretext of the war against drugs, the US has been able to play an active role in the vast atrocities conducted by the security forces and their paramilitary associates in Colombia, now the leading human rights violator in Latin America, and now the leading recipient of US aid and training, increasing under Clinton — again, no surprise in the real world. The war against drugs is 'a myth', Amnesty International reports, agreeing with other investigators. Security forces work closely with narcotraffickers and landlords while targeting the usual victims, including community leaders, human rights and health workers, union activists, students, the political opposition, but primarily peasants, in a country where protest has been criminalised.

Subsequent International Covenants are respected in much the manner of the UD. The Convention on the Rights of the Child has been ratified by 159 countries, including every country of the Americas apart from the USA. After delaying for decades, it did endorse the International Covenant on Civil and Political Rights, 'the leading treaty for the protection' of the narrow category of rights that the West claims to uphold, observe Human Rights Watch and the American Civil Liberties Union in their report on US non-compliance with its provisions*. The Bush administration ensured that the treaty would be inoperative by eliminating provisions that might expand rights and declaring the US in full compliance with the remaining ones. The treaty is 'non-self-executing' and accompanied by no enabling legislation, so it cannot be invoked in US courts and ratification was 'an empty act for Americans,' the HRW/ACLU report continues.

As the most powerful state, the USA makes its own laws, using force and conducting sermonic warfare at will.

The exceptions are crucial, because the US violates the treaty 'in important respects,' the report observes, giving numerous examples. To cite one, the US entered a specific reservation to Article 7, which states that 'No one shall be subjected to torture or to cruel, inhuman, or degrading treatment or punishment.' The reason is that conditions in prisons in the USA — which leads the world in imprisoning its population, the numbers almost tripling during the Reagan years — violate these conditions as generally understood, just as they seriously violate the provisions of Article 10 on humane treatment of prisoners and on the right to 'reformation and social rehabilitation,' which the US flatly rejects. Another US reservation concerns the death penalty, which is not only employed far more freely than the norm but also 'applied in a manner that is racially discriminatory,' the HRW/ACLU report observes, reiterating the conclusions of many studies.

Other International Covenants submitted to Congress also were restricted as 'non-self-executing.' In the case of the UN Convention Against Torture and Other Forms of Cruel, Inhuman or Degrading Treatment or Punishment, the Senate imposed this restriction, in part to protect a Supreme Court ruling allowing corporal punishment in schools.

The USA is a world leader in defence of freedom of speech, perhaps unique in realising Enlightenment values at least since the 1960s. With regard to civil-political rights and 'anti-torture' rights, the US record at home ranks well by comparative standards, though a serious evaluation would have to take into account the capacity to uphold such rights, including the extraordinary advantages the country has enjoyed from its origins. The social and economic provisions of the UD and other conventions are operative only insofar as popular struggle over many years has given them substance. The point generalises; as James Madison observed, a 'parchment barrier' will not protect freedom and rights. The earlier record within the national territory is hideous, and the human rights record abroad is a scandal, though it has somewhat improved as popular forces have placed limits on state terror.

But the realities are for the most part 'kept dark, without any need for any official ban,' much as Orwell understood.

* *Human rights violations in the United States: a report on US compliance with the International Covenant on Civil and Political Rights* (Human Rights Watch/American Civil Liberties Union, December 1993)

NEWS REVIEW

BECHIR ZNAGIE

The voyage perilous

Europe too has its boat people: a tragic tide flowing from North Africa and further south

On 20 May this year, two bodies were fished from the sea off the coast of Tangiers by the Moroccan gendarmerie. They were identified as members of a group of nine men who had disappeared on 6 May when a small boat went down in the Straits of Gibraltar. Of the 22 who embarked secretly that night from the Tangiers beach en route for the Spanish coast, 10 are now known to have drowned in the course of a violent storm with 10-feet high waves which capsized the boat. Seven of the passengers, including the owner of the boat, escaped back to Morocco where they were picked up by the security forces. The owner, already known to the Moroccan police since being identified by members of earlier cargos who had been arrested on Spanish soil, is one of many who offer their services to those seeking to enter Europe illegally. Their small boats, fitted with outboard motors and known by the Spanish as *pateras,* are unsuited for the crossing and disasters are a regular occurrence. For the most part, the illegal immigrants, as well as those who perish in the attempt, are Moroccan. Embarrassed by Spanish criticism and by the parallels drawn between the *pateras* and the Asian boat people, the Moroccan authorities attempt to keep the fact to themselves and have increased coastal policing in an effort to stop the traffic. Despite this, numbers have been swollen in recent years by would-be immigrants from other Mahgreb countries and from Sub-Saharan Africa.

It would be an exaggeration to talk of a continent-wide network, but there is little doubt that foreigners from across the continent, inspired, perhaps, by tales of the lucky few who have reached their destination, are drawn from considerable distances to places like Tangiers and Tétouan, simply to be in sight of the promised land.

Last year, the villagers from Fquih Ben Salah achieved brief notoriety when a number of their young men lost their lives in the crossing. Successive years of drought have reduced the region to a desert and emptied it of its population. Young men seduced by the 'Italian myth' relayed back home by the 'success' of neighbours who have made the voyage, are tempted to venture on the near impossible journey. Families sell everything, livestock and land, to finance the venture. At least a dozen more young men have died or been captured by the Spanish and Moroccan authorities, most of them from rural areas badly hit by drought and poverty. Unemployed youth from Casablanca, who have given up any hope of a visa, are adding to the clandestine exit, many in the hope of joining friends and family already illegally installed in southern Europe — France, Spain and Italy.

The Spanish and Moroccan media have presented the owners of the *pateras* as big-time criminals. More often than not they are one-time fishermen and seamen who, having lost their old livelihood in the general economic destitution of northern Morocco, have turned to small-time smuggling, drug trafficking and ferrying of illegal immigrants. Their only asset is a knowledge of the treacherous waters of the Straits which they confront — and in which they frequently perish — with their passengers in the dead of night. The real mafia, the big drug barons, are equipped with power boats and high-speed launches to carry their cargoes of marijuana into Europe, and have no interest in the slim pickings from human cargoes.

The illegal traffic in the *pateras* is nothing new: in the 1960s the boats carried seasonal workers and migrants from the Rif going to work in the Andalucian fishing fleet or as agricultural labourers. The only reason they were reduced to clandestine travel was the Moroccan government's refusal to grant passports. What has changed in recent years is the volley of new legislation in Europe that makes the work of the *pateras* more difficult and more dangerous though no less in demand.

In the 1960s, the *pateras* ferried their passengers out to sea where they were transferred to larger vessels and landed openly at small ports on the Andalucian coast. Since then the Moroccan maritime police have been given speed boats to patrol the Straits and pick up the *pateras*. More rigid controls at European consulates in Morocco have resulted in the refusal of visas to more than 90 per cent of applicants. Legal sanctions against vessels which pick up illegals at sea mean that given the steady demand for their services, the *pateras* must attempt to reach the Spanish coast under their own power. Despite the dangers and the expense, the flow of illegal immigrants continues to grow, Africans as well as Moroccans.

PETER ELAM

Hoist on its own media

The struggle over the state-run Hungarian Radio and Television (HRTV) has continued to dominate political debates. Last-ditch attempts by the government to fill the airwaves with propaganda in order to avert a humiliating electoral defeat in the general elections in May backfired.

Since taking over Hungarian Radio and Television in April 1993, and despite massive public protests against government interference in HRTV, Laszlo Csucs and Gabor Nahlik have axed news programmes, such as *Egyenleg* (Evening Balance) and *Thought and Sign*, and dismissed over 120 journalists *(Index* 7/1993, 1&2/1994).

It seems clear that the suspensions of *Egyenleg* journalists were politically motivated. Zsolt Deak, the Hungarian Television lawyer chosen by Nahlik to investigate allegations that *Egyenleg* journalists falsified a news report, resigned in December 1993. In a radio interview on 8 January 1994 Deak said that in his view the *Egyenleg* report was genuine, and that Nahlik had tried to bribe him to say otherwise. Given that around US$1 million was paid out in severance pay and programmes already made by the sacked journalists were not broadcast, the economic reasons cited by Csucs for the sacking of Hungarian Radio journalists are equally dubious. Allegations that Csucs and Nahlik are acting out of sympathy with far-right elements pushed out of the government coalition in 1993, rather than on behalf of the government itself are rife. According to a radio report on 22 April, Csucs stated that radio journalists sacked on 4 March were selected on the basis of purported pre-1989 links to the Communist Party and secret police.

Others see present events as part of a long term plan. According to radio journalist Miklos Gyorffy, 'The right within the government has led on media issues since 1990.' 'When the government wants to intervene,

they invoke the 1974 media law; when they don't want to admit they are interfering, they say they cannot intervene.' Hungarian Radio and Television have remained in a legal vacuum, filled only partly by the 1974 regulations since parliament's four-year-long failure to pass a Media Law. The moratorium on allocating national radio and television frequencies stands.

The government appears to have misjudged the effects of its propaganda: attacks on the Socialist Party have backfired. An edition of the television programme *Panorama*, highlighting Socialist leader Gyula Horn's role in the Communist workers' militia that helped crush the 1956 uprising, drew him much sympathy. And despite warnings by the main weekly television news review *The Week*, that voters should be wary of the 'liberal-bolshevik alliance' and the 'mass murderers' waiting to take over the country, the liberals and Socialists together took over half of the popular vote in the first round of elections on 8 May, and won an overall majority in the second round on 29 May.

The Socialists and Free Democrats, who seem likely to form a coalition government, both put the passage of a Media Law high on their agenda, and deny any intention to carry out counter-purges in HRTV. There are also plans to privatise one of the three national radio channels, and open up the airwaves to new frequencies.

Not everyone is optimistic. 'My fear is that those who did leave in

1989 will creep back,' says Gyorffy. Many, such as Istvan Schlett, Professor of Political Science at Eotvos University in Budapest, believe that the years of failing to reach a consensus has left a deep rift in the media and Hungarian intellectual life that will not easily be bridged.

But the message from Eastern Europe is, overall, a positive one. Predictions that the ruling coalition would win votes because of their dominance of radio and TV were disproved by their resounding defeat. But after over 40 years of Communist propaganda, voters are highly sceptical of attempts to manipulate them through the media. Whether governments will take heed is a different matter.

GENEVIEVE HESSE

Hi-tech terror

Threats from neo-Nazis are forcing German journalists to choose self-defence or self-censorship

Burkhard Schröder, a freelance journalist who has been following the activities of the far right since 1988, now goes to work armed. He is one of the prime targets of the neo-Nazis. Last summer, the *Staatsschutz* — the police department in charge of counter-subversion — advised him to arm himself and provided the usually hard-to-come-by licence. 'Apart from the standard death threats by phone and in the post, I've never actually been attacked. They'll never get me: my flat's hard to get into.'

However, he has taken some serious protective measures: a PO box number instead of his address; a metal detector to check for letter-bombs. Schröder does, in fact, have something to worry about. Last December the neo-Nazi publication *Der Einblick* published his photo and that of the photographer he works with, Dietmar Gust, as well as a list of people, several journalists among them, for whom it predicted 'sleepless nights'. 'Any small-time neo-Nazi knows my face now. I can't hang around the clubs the young people go to; I've absolutely no intention of courting danger.' In March 1992, in Dresden, Dietmar Gust narrowly escaped a neo-Nazis knife attack by leaping into a taxi. Schröder has not attempted any further research in the area since.

Schröder is not the only journalist to have felt the pressure, particularly since reunification. 'Neo-Nazi efficiency has improved dramatically now that they're using an electronic communications network. My face can be transmitted overnight to the other end of Germany where they can get one of their members to check out the layout of my office, to see if I've got any windows,' says Franziska Hundseder, a member of the *Presserat* (Press Council) specialising in the far right for TV. She also writes in *Stern* and *Die Zeit*. Death threats were already part of her work before reunification, but since the Wall came down, things have got worse. 'There are a lot more neo-Nazis around and they're bolder. I find stickers on my door. That never used to happen.'

In the West, few journalists admit to intimidation. Schröder has kept the tape from his answering machine with the threats recorded at least once a month: 'This is Germany on the line, you filthy lefty swine. We'll get rid of you. I hope for your sake you've taken out good comprehensive insurance.'

Most journalists see the new danger as no more than an occupational hazard. 'If you get involved in politics, you make enemies. If you set out to expose the Nazis, you make dangerous enemies,' says Klaus Farin in an article in *Die Tageszeitung*. 'Blacks crossing Friedrichshain (a district in East Berlin) run greater risks every day. Only three or four members of the press are in real physical danger. The real danger is the lack of fighting spirit in our profession.'

The Berlin police feel much the same. 'We have no record of a journalist falling victim to the Nazis. The death threats are almost always empty. If journalists are upset maybe they haven't chosen the right profession,' says Harald C, official of the *Staatsschutz* in charge of dealing with the far right and racism in Berlin. He advises journalists to go ex-directory and not to use their own cars when covering demonstrations by the far right. 'The incidence of violence hasn't increased among the far right, except among the young,' he claims, but does acknowledge that their computer network and the list of

'You wanna take my photo?'
'Sure. Ah well... mm... p'raps not.'

names adds 'another dimension to the physical threat'.

The latter is most apparent in small towns in Eastern Germany and targets the editorial staff of local papers. Sandra Dabler, a journalist with *Lausitzer Rundschau* in Cottbus, comments: 'Unlike the West we weren't used to death threats. Now it's become routine, so we use pseudonyms. Some of my colleagues go in for a kind of self-censorship. They've asked themselves if it's worth writing on the far right if it puts their children in danger. However, there have been a lot less threats in the last year and a half.'

During a seminar in Bonn she met a journalist whose 15-year-old son had been attacked in the street. His mother had defended foreigners in the local paper. She was forced to leave the town. Sandra Dabler recalls that in 1991 and 1992 journalists in the East had the added problem of the sale of their paper to new press groups. 'Why would they take such risks at a time when they didn't even know if they would still have their jobs next month?'

At *Murkishe Oderzeitung* in Schwedt nobody covers the far right. The journalist prepared to talk insists on anonymity: 'Speaking out can be provocative. To say we are frightened would be an exaggeration. Some of us sometimes use pseudonyms, sure, but not just because of the far right. I can assure you we don't avoid writing about things.' When asked about death threats and neo-Nazi pressure, she was taken aback. 'Thank God, we haven't had anything like that here yet. Mind you, last summer our offices were covered with far right slogans but we contacted the police and it was all removed. Since that we haven't really had any trouble here. '

Walter Wullenweber, a Western journalist on the *Berliner Zeitung*, lives in what was formerly the city's eastern zone. He has no sympathy for local journalists used to the old eastern press: 'They're cowards, not worth the name journalist. The fact that they've taken no action is an enormous help to the far right. They're not used to a free press and don't realise that it's never given freely but always has to be fought for.'

Yet Wullenweber does not deny the danger in places like Schwedt: last summer skinheads threatened to beat him up in a café in Schwedt. Twenty marks and an appeal to 'national honour' got him out of the mess; local police support, he says, was not impressive. Wullenweber now uses a hire car when he visits Schwedt and, following police advice, is planning to move 'to a flat that's harder to break into'.

Rainer Weisflog, a photographer with the *Deutsche Presseagentur* (DPA) in Cottbus, another victim of neo-Nazi violence, was not let off as lightly as Wullenweber. 'Five neo-Nazis set upon me: some held me down, others threw stones. The same night, after being stitched up at the hospital, I went back to where it had all happened. The police wanted to stop me taking photographs: they were set on arresting the witnesses and letting the perpetrators of the violence get away. I was trapped between the neo-Nazis and the police — who did not come to our aid, quite the opposite.

'My tripod can be used as a weapon and I have a gas gun in my car. I can't afford to take risks: *Deutsche Alternative* — the banned far -right organisation — know where I live with my family. When I took photographs of the head of the DA as the police were arresting him outside his house, he said, 'Don't print that, you'll be sorry.' I was going to 'phone the agency and tell them I'd got exclusive photos but another of DA's leaders threatened me again as I was making the call from a call-box. 'Think what you're doing,' he warned, and I suggested a different photo.'

Translated from La Lettre de Reporters sans Frontières *by Carmen Gibson*
Peter Johnson adds: The latest figures

issued by the Cologne-based federal office for the Protection of the Constitution (OPC) showed a 15 per cent fall in violent offences by right-wing extremists in 1993 compared with 1992. They indicated that the downward trend has accelerated this year.

Political observers say the likely reasons include: improved policing, particularly in eastern Germany where police forces are being reorganised following reunification; severer sentences by the courts; the economic upturn in eastern Germany; and increased realisation by the public and in the media of the need for firm action against right-wing violence.

An anti-crime bill pending in the Bundestag includes a passage, almost certain to be approved, introducing speedier and tougher sentencing for incitement to racial hatred.

MILICA PESIC

Breaking the information blockade

After the breakup of the former Yugoslavia and the ensuing war, communications in the region were severely disrupted. The Alternative Information Network (AIM), a computer network of independent journalists based in different centres in the new republics, was set up in October 1992 to combat these restrictions.

Since going on-line in June 1993, AIM has operated daily, circulating information between its different centres via the main office in Paris. Articles from AIM have been published in various independent media including *Arkzin* and *Feral Tribune* in Croatia, *Vreme* and *Borba* in Serbia, *Monitor* in Montenegro, and *Koha* in Kosovo. One of AIM's objectives is also to support existing independent media in the republics and to provide at least some work for journalists who lost their jobs when they refused to participate in the propaganda war. Access is given free of charge to independent media but withheld from official media that follow their respective republic's nationalist line.

AIM is hoping to encourage foreign media to use its material. An information service for media, institutions and non-government organisations inside and outside former Yugoslavia is provided, and every fortnight a selection of articles is published in English in the *AIM Review*.

Information available from AIM, 13 Rue Gazan, S-75014, Paris, France tel (331) 45 89 89 49 fax (331) 45 80 99 40; or c/o WarReport, 33 Islington High Street, London N1 9LH

BOB SUTCLIFFE

Migration, rights and illogic

'Every age has its
Inquisition. Our age
has the passport to
make up for the torture
of mediaeval times.
And unemployment.'

B Traven, *The Death Ship*, 1925

(Left) Kurdish refugee 1992: asylum denied: Deutsche Presse-Agentur/Camera Press
(Above) Point of arrival 1989: Welcome to your new home: Sven Simon/Camera Press

More than 100 million people around the world are today living in countries of which they are not citizens. At least 40 million migrants have moved from South to North in recent years, primarily in search of work; a further 20 million are international refugees; and 23 million are displaced in their own countries. They constitute at least 2 per cent of the world's population and their numbers are growing. Yet not only do constitutions, laws and governments restrict their rights to move freely, to speak and to be heard, the present structure of recognised human rights provides no framework within which the rights of migrants — including the right to speak and to be heard — can be discussed.

Countries such as Afghanistan, Somalia, Burundi, Nicaragua or Guatemala are among those that have lost the greatest percentage of their population to emigration, while Malawi, Iran, Sudan, the USA and Germany number the most immigrants in proportion to their own population. According to UN statistics, which refer only to official refugees, Europe has 4.39 million refugees — approximately 25 per cent of the total.

Migrants fall into many categories: refugees from persecution, ethnic violence, famine, natural or ecological disaster, searchers for family, friends, sexual freedom, peace, money, work, culture, excitement and many other things. Their migrations can be categorised along various axes: from forced to voluntary migrations; from small to large distance migrations (where distance can be viewed as geographical or social); and from economic to non-economic migrations. In spite of these contrasts and the great variety of theoretical and ideological standpoints, two features are common to nearly all discourses on migration: an implicitly or explicitly hostile attitude to migration and the clash between the logic applied to migration and that applied to other questions.

Nowhere is this more evident than in the treatment of migration within the received wisdom on human rights. When it comes to migration, the existing human rights orthodoxy displays a profound — perhaps an absurd — contradiction. The Universal Declaration of Human Rights concedes the right to be a citizen of a country, to be free to move within that country, not to have a passport of that country withheld, to leave and re-enter that country at will and without restriction. And then — silence.

According to this statement of rights, we have a universal human right to depart but not to arrive. Arrival is regarded as a privilege which each nation state can withhold or disburse on the grounds of political expediency or any other criterion unrelated to human rights. Only a few countries impose restrictions on emigration; all, without exception, seek to control immigration.

Asylum for *bona fide* political refugees is, however, accepted as a universal human right in many countries — in Europe, for instance, where the post-war realisation that the lack of a right of refuge for Jews and others contributed to Nazi genocide in the 1930s and 1940s — but these rights are now being severely curtailed, thus severing even this tenuous connection between immigration and rights.

This makes an examination of the attitudes surrounding migration increasingly important: the number of migrants obliged to, or choosing to move is growing fast and their living conditions are among the worst in the world. In some political contexts migrants are being blamed for all manner of social ills and coming under physical attack.

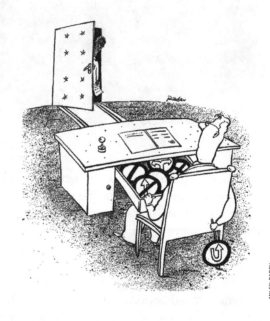

MILEN RADEV

Efforts to justify the exclusion of the right to immigration from the list of human rights are unpersuasive. Philosophers searching for a rational justification for restrictions on immigration tend to come up with the analogy between a nation and a household. Since it is generally recognised that existing members of a household should have the right to leave, but that other people do not have the right to enter without the

Hungary 1992: camp for illegal immigrants

existing occupants' consent, the same should apply to nations.

However, though purporting to be an explanation, this argument fails entirely to make logical sense of the existing list of basic human rights since movement within a country is regarded as a human right. If the home is a suitable analogy for a country, it must also be a suitable analogy for a village, a city or a province. Yet apparently no-one argues that the citizens of Kingston UK should have the right to control the entry of the citizens of neighbouring Surbiton. Either the home analogy is invalid or it would legitimise all exclusions, not only national ones.

In any case, the right of a nation state to restrict entry has another anomaly: the borders of nation states are the result of historical accidents and frequently change. It is an odd concept of universal human rights which concludes that a person has the right to migrate from Prague to Bratislava in 1991 (movement within a nation state) but not in 1993 (movement between nation states). It would seem that the only way to bring logical coherence to the treatment of the rights to move is either to remove all rights or to add the missing right, that of immigration: to reduce or expand the existing list.

There is little association between the human rights enshrined in the Universal Declaration and what actually happens in the world. The fact that it is a universal human right to have a job and enough to eat has not eliminated unemployment or hunger. But the declaration of these concepts as rights helps define, however loosely, some shared concept of what is desirable and acceptable. Such rights can serve to legitimise and also to de-legitimise: political leaders do not say that their policy is to increase unemployment or to make people starve, even if that is what they really intend. Which is not to say that hypocrisy is a good idea, only that some shared concept of what is acceptable in human affairs may have positive effects; discourse occasionally has the power to legitimise.

Because it is missing from the list of recognised human rights, immigration has almost no such rules of acceptable discourse. With the partial exception of the right to political asylum, it is not illegitimate in relation to any human rights document for a minister to say that he or she advocates 'zero immigration' as did French minister Charles Pasqua, hard on the heels of his government's entering office in 1993. In relation to recognised human rights, that exception is an anomaly expressing a hierarchy or prioritisation of human rights.

Certain political rights — to opposition, to vote, to freedom of speech, to not suffer arbitrary detention etc — have become virtually synonymous with human rights in general. The absence of these rights in a country is what justifies the right to political asylum: people become political refugees because they lack human rights in their country of citizenship. No such right of asylum, however, is ever mentioned in relation to the violation of other recognised universal human rights, such as the right to employment or adequate nutrition. In fact, in Western Europe in recent years, exactly the opposite has happened. A distinction is increasingly being made between the 'good' migrants who are fleeing political persecution and 'bad' migrants who are simply looking for a materially better life and who have been, in the words of the Moroccan writer Tahar Ben Jelloun, 'demonised' by politicians. This demonisation has served to cast suspicion on all migrants, the majority of whom are officially seen as economic migrants fraudulently posing as political refugees. The distinction has been used to justify the recent changes in European laws and constitutions and as the basis for the forced repatriation of Vietnamese boat people by the Hong Kong/British government. The USA, which roundly condemns Hong Kong, does precisely the same to Haitian migrants.

The lack of logic in the distinction made between people fleeing a lack of political and a lack of economic rights highlights another curious contradiction. The neo-liberal economic counter-revolution, which has so universally affected economic ideas and policy since the end of the 1970s, has stressed, in addition to free trade and free capital movement, the importance of personal responsibility, self-reliance, self-help and the need for flexible labour markets (included in this is geographical flexibility). The 'economic migrant' would seem to be a perfect example of the market virtues we are now exhorted to admire. But it appears that even in these days of globalisation, when goods and money move freely, the labour market must stop at the frontier.

The resulting inequalities are twofold: while the products of human labour have acquired a freedom to move, their human creators have no such freedom; and, in practice, the latter right operates on a differential scale closely related to the amount of money they have. Bankers and other capitalists move relatively freely, as do some kinds of highly skilled workers; unskilled workers are usually denied that freedom.

Despite such anomalies, even the most doctrinaire free market economists, although they are sometimes on the liberal end of the immigration debate, hesitate to go the whole way and advocate free movement of people. On your bike, as Margaret Thatcher's minister Norman Tebbit said, and you are a saint shining with neo-liberal virtues. On your ferry, and you are a demon against whom great European democracies change their constitutions in panic.

Most migration occurs not under the rubric of right, but either under the pressure of utter necessity or haphazardly under the rubric of inconsistent laws and opportunities. Not all migrants lose human and political rights when they leave their countries of origin since in many cases few such rights exist. Nonetheless, migration under present rules is a process which tends to reduce the sum of human rights since immigrants, even if they acquire legal rights to residence, have fewer rights than already-resident populations. Often, their presence is conditional on good behaviour, they cannot vote, and they may not receive social benefits. Although in principle human rights are considered universal they have juridical force only within the frontiers of a nation state and are closely associated with citizenship.

As a result, even the most liberal regimes tend to reduce the total of juridical and/or political rights of migrants. For instance, citizens of the countries of the European Union have acquired rights of travel, residence and employment in any country of the Union. However, legal residents of the 12 member countries who are not also citizens, do not have any of these rights. When Union citizens register a change of national residence they transfer some of their rights: they can join the social security system and they can vote in local and European parliamentary elections in their countries of residence. They may not, however, vote in national parliamentary elections nor become state functionaries. The *reductio ad absurdam* of this situation is that if all European Union citizens were to take advantage of their new rights to migrate within the Union, no-one

would any longer be able to vote for national governments. Or, to put it more reasonably, the more people move, the less will be the proportion of the ruled population to whom a national government is electorally answerable.

The only thing which would stop migration leading to a steady erosion of rights and democratic controls is for immigrants rapidly to acquire political and other rights, preferably through easy access to citizenship. Yet naturalisation is everywhere difficult, the rules governing it in most places are tightening and many countries make ethnic origin a condition of naturalisation, something which excludes most immigrants from full rights for ever. Immigrants to the USA acquire rights much more quickly than immigrants to the European Union and, since they are often considered part of the electorate to which politicians are answerable, carry much more political weight. This is almost never true in the European Union where immigrants are treated as spectators who, like Victorian children, should be seen and not heard.

Given this absence of any recognised right to be where they are, immigrants are in a juridical situation in which, before naturalisation, they have, at best, fewer rights than full citizens. Many, however, are not so lucky. They may fall into the black hole of human rights which has developed at the borders of the main receiving countries. Would-be migrants who are stopped at border controls risk interrogation and search, a spell in a transit camp with no contact with the rest of the world and forcible repatriation, all under conditions of which the general public is seldom aware. They have no right to a lawyer nor opportunity to contact anyone who could help them. Temporary camps and residences can be as inaccessible as military establishments and agitation on detainees' behalf is often impossible because their fate is a well-kept secret. Their absence of rights inevitably brings with it a reduction in the rights of existing residents to know what happens in the country where they live. It is never possible to reduce the rights of one group without at the same time eroding those of all.

Nearly all political economists see immigration primarily in the context of the labour market where capitalists have exploited migrant labour to weaken the bargaining power of national labour. The implicit bias against immigration seen here extends to the world of development studies where the brain-drain has been regarded as a disaster and the remittances of migrants — which now amount to more than all development aid and are second only to oil as an export earner for the Third World — are generally regarded as bad for the economy and blamed for raising imports, consumption and inflation. New ideas about human development may, perhaps, be changing this bias given growing concern with the freedom of individuals to meet their needs, and less precoccupation with territorially-based economic aggregates.

Yet another area which has come to develop an anti-immigration discourse is ecology. In the USA, prominent ecologists and environmental protection organisations have recently made the restriction of immigration into a major part of their argument for ecological protection. In his recent book, *Living Within Limits: Ecology, Economics and Population Taboos*, Garrett Hardin proposes draconian restrictions on immigration to prevent the Third World exporting its population problem to the USA.

Why does the unconditional freedom of human beings to move freely in the planet they inhabit have so little support? Given the lack of rational arguments showing that the volume of migration resulting from the freedom to move would have negative consequences for the sending countries, the receiving countries and the migrants themselves, much opposition is based on irrational prejudice that expresses itself in xenophobia and racism.

The apparently non-racist arguments are a combination of the sincere and the insincere. When Jean-Marie Le Pen publicly worries for the poor conditions in which many immigrants live we may safely assume that he is being insincere. Even when the arguments are sincere, much of the concern is due to confusion, such as fear that immigration is associated with ills such as unemployment, an increase in crime and homelessness as demonstrated in Holland during the recent election campaign.

Bosnia 1992: Secret refugee camp

However, comparison of the countries of the European Union shows that those with fewer immigrants tend to have more unemployment. The fear that immigration will lower the bargaining power of labour in receiving countries has much more basis in relation to illegal than legal immigration, since illegal migrants are super-exploitable because of the threat of discovery and deportation. Restrictions on immigration justified by their effect on the labour market tend to have perverse results; unless enforced with fascist rigour they are likely to increase the number of illegal migrants. Illegality rather than migration is the problem.

In other respects, some of the problems which are attributed to immigration are the result of the neglect of real social and economic problems by governments. The feeling against immigration is likely to grow in periods such as the present age of neo-liberal economics when governments fail to tackle the fundamental causes of social problems. Immigration does not create the conflict; it merely changes the way it manifests itself — and immigrants become popular scapegoats for government failure.

The lack of clear thinking on immigration and the growing anti-immigration bias in social and political discourse have given strength to the racist posture. In recent years we have seen it diffusing by insidious osmosis through the whole political fabric. Yesterday, racists burn down the houses of immigrants; today a Social Democrat politician says we are close to the 'threshold of tolerance' — of immigrants, not of racists; tomorrow the constitution is changed; will the size of the police force be doubled the day after tomorrow to stop the flow of illegal migrants?

It will not be easy to stop that trajectory. But you do not have to believe in the unfettered power of ideology or logic to believe that part of the problem is the almost universal failure to regard the freedom to move as a basic human right. Liberal and progressive positions on immigration are weakened by having no sure vision of what is ultimately desirable and just. The logical confusions which this produces mean that they are inevitably forced into defensive positions when racists attack. If there is no universal right to migrate then what the racists are saying is not, measured against declared universal human values, so awful: it is simply an extreme position in a politically acceptable debate. Counter-osmosis needs to be based on an equally clear statement of an ideal.

If there existed in the world a country in which various ethnic groups lived, and in which the richest and most powerful group divided the country into ethnic areas, forbade the poorer, less powerful groups to enter the privileged groups' areas, except under strict conditions where they had to carry passes and submit to constant and humiliating police controls, which would often result in forced removals, then there is a good chance that is would be declared a pariah by other nations for its denial of human rights. Such a country did, until very recently, exist: South Africa under apartheid. And it was universally — if, by some, hypocritically — condemned. Yet, viewed as a whole, the world is worse in these respects than South Africa under apartheid. On the right to move, and the right of migrants when they have moved, the world is a macrocosm of the country which all other countries found impossible to accept. The freedom to migrate — an end to the world pass laws — would be an essential plank in an anti-apartheid movement for the world.

Based on the 1993 Jon Lopategui Memorial Lecture delivered by the author at Kingston University on 16 November 1993. Jon Lopategui, whose family migrated to Britain from the Basque Country during the Spanish Civil War, was my friend and colleague in the Economics and Politics Department, Kingston Polytechnic during the 1970s and 1980s. He died in 1989.

SHADA ISLAM

Fortress Europe

The term used only a few years ago to describe the European Union's protectionist strategy to keep out competing foreign goods and services, has become charged with a more sinister meaning

T ROZSAHEGYI/CAMERA PRESS

The 12 states of the European Union, using Brussels' single-market programme as a convenient pretext, are creating a closed, inward-looking Europe where new visa regulations, immigration laws and asylum rules are being designed and implemented to keep out people as well as

East to West Germany: rites of passage

television sets and cars.

The new 'fortress' is being built, at least partly, in secret. Although the Maastricht Treaty on political union signed in 1991 recognises for the first time that immigration is a matter of 'common interest' for EU governments, most of the regular EU meetings on immigration and asylum policies are still held with a minimum of publicity. While immigration is an issue that governments are anxious to talk about among themselves, they prefer not to be overheard.

Yet, the signs of hardening attitudes towards immigrants and refugees cannot be missed. Not in France, where interior minister Charles Pasqua has said that France will refuse to accept any 'wave' of refugees fleeing Algeria if the Islamic Salvation Front takes power. Not in Germany, where the government is under attack for not taking tougher action against right-wing groups that continue to terrorise immigrants and foreign refugees. Not in Britain, which has just tightened its immigration rules for overseas students and casual workers.

The stringent rules are a response to the EU's increasing fears of a looming immigration 'crisis'. The concern dates back to 1989 and the collapse of the Berlin Wall when, over the space of just a few months, over a million people surged across the borders from Eastern to Western Europe. The fears of an exodus from the east have been compounded in recent months by apprehension about events on the EU's southern flank. France, Spain, Portugal and Italy have told EU authorities in Brussels they are not ready to accept refugees fleeing religious extremism and economic difficulties in North Africa.

As political, ethnic and economic problems multiply across their borders, EU countries which once stuck adamantly to their national competence in the area of immigration are coming to the conclusion they can no longer go it alone. Hence the Maastricht decision to take joint action on the issue.

'We have a long way to go,' admits an aide to the European Commissioner for Social Affairs, Padraig Flynn. 'Member states still have a great deal of muscle when it comes to immigration and asylum issues. The European Commission is limited in what it can do.'

But change is in the air. Under the Maastricht Treaty, EU member states have, for the first time, agreed to cooperate on justice and home affairs within the Union framework. Policy on migration is touched by each of the three pillars of the Treaty.

A new Article 100C, inserted into the first pillar (community matters under the Treaty of Rome), states that the Council of the European Community 'shall determine the third countries whose nationals must be in possession of a visa when crossing the external borders of the member states.' Before 1 January 1996, member states 'shall adopt the measures related to uniform format for visas,' it adds.

The first article of the third pillar (intergovernmental cooperation in justice and home affairs), is more wide-ranging, listing areas which member states shall regard as 'matters of common interest'. These include policy on asylum, rules governing the crossing of external borders and immigration. Policy on nationals of third countries, in particular conditions of entry, movement and residence are also affected.

The second pillar (foreign and security policy), while not explicitly related to migration, does deal indirectly with the issue since the movement of people has become increasingly intertwined with wider political and security issues — as in the exodus from former Yugoslavia.

'The commitment in the Maastricht Treaty to cooperation on a permanent basis constitutes a considerable political signal both to public opinion in member states and to the outside world,' the European Commission claims. It also claims that immigration will be discussed within a more rational, more stratified and more coordinated structure than in the past.

In the 1950s and 1960s, EU nations were active recruiters of migrant labour. By the 1970s, however, most had stopped seeking out guest workers and introduced restrictive immigration policies. According to EC figures, the number of new, non-EU immigrants arriving in the Union dropped from 1.3 million in 1991 to 274,789 in 1992. The main source of this immigration is the arrival of family members joining workers already in Europe.

Europe's first attempts to coordinate immigration policy can be traced back to 1976 when the Trevi group of interior ministers was set up at the instigation of the UK to enable countries to cooperate on dealing with terrorism. The group expanded its brief in the mid-1980s to embrace the policing and security aspects of free movement including immigration, visas, asylum-seekers and border controls.

Trevi has worked on the basis of shared information on migratory flows, clandestine immigration networks and forged documents. With its informal discussions and secret agreements far from the scrutiny of the European Parliament or even national parliaments, the group has served as a model for the development of common immigration and asylum policies.

The single market plan launched by the European Commission in 1985 triggered a new focus on the problem of controlling the Union's external borders. It was clear, officials said, that if Europe's 'internal' frontiers were to be dismantled, new rules would be needed to make sure that the controls at their shared external borders were as reliable as the ones they would be losing on the frontiers between them. While EU citizens would retain the 'privileges' of free movement, others were to be kept out.

The first joint initiative, the 'Ad Hoc Immigration Group' of senior officials, was set up by ministers responsible for immigration in October 1986. Its first two endeavours were the Dublin Convention on asylum, which sets out rules for the examination of asylum requests, and the draft convention on crossing the EU's external borders.

The Dublin Convention, which has been signed but not ratified, prevents asylum seekers from making multiple or successive applications in more than one EU country and is an attempt to deal with the problem of refugees who are forced into orbit when no one country will accept responsibility for them. The draft convention on crossing the Union's external borders remains unsigned because of the dispute between Spain and the UK over Gibraltar. It aims to apply uniform standards to immigration. A list of countries whose citizens need visas to travel in the EU has been drawn up and the convention provides for member states to recognise each others' visas.

Towards the end of 1991, member states began to look beyond their joint obsession with the flow of would-be immigrants into the Community, and jointly to scrutinise other aspects of immigration policy for the first time.

Responding to this change in attitudes, the European Commission drew up its first comprehensive document on immigration. The report drew attention to the link between immigration and asylum, pointing out the danger for genuine asylum seekers should asylum come to be seen as a back-door to immigration.

In parallel with the EU's struggle to cooperate on the issue, in 1985 France and Germany joined Belgium, the Netherlands and Luxembourg in signing the Schengen agreement. This extended the decades-old Benelux border-free zone. In 1990 Italy joined the accord, followed by Spain and Portugal in 1991 and Greece in 1992.

The Schengen agreement is seen as a laboratory for what the EU states could achieve. The nine countries have drawn up a common list of 120 countries whose nationals require entry visas, and cooperate on the exchange of information on combating illegal immigration and drug trafficking. Plans to abolish all identity checks at their common borders have been delayed until later this year because of technical problems.

All EU countries, except Ireland, which has no formal refugee procedures, now have in place measures for turning back refugees who come via another EU country and for 'accelerated processing' of 'manifestly unfounded' refugees. All have a form of detention for some asylum seekers in prisons, barracks, camps, reception centres and ships; most have instituted lower levels of welfare benefits for asylum seekers, together with a ban on working during all or part of the assessment procedure.

Such measures have been backed with other deterrents such as sanctions on carriers that transport would-be immigrants and fingerprinting. Germany closed its doors in May 1993, capitulating to its racists by changing the constitutional right to asylum. Asylum-seekers can now be sent back to countries deemed safe.

Throughout Europe, family reunion rights are also being squeezed, with the maximum age for the entry of dependent children moving steadily downwards and the right made subject in more and more countries to stiff financial maintenance and accommodation criteria.

Acting under the new authority given to the European Commissioner under the Maastricht Treaty, Social Affairs Commissioner Flynn has taken the first tentative steps toward hammering out a long-term 'strategy' on immigration and asylum.

His new 'communication' to ministers in February 1994 stresses that immigration is not a 'temporary phenomenon'. 'More importantly, immigration has been a positive process which has brought economic and broader cultural benefits both to the host countries and the immigrants themselves,' Flynn underlined. 'The concerns about mass movements of people towards Western Europe from the ex-Soviet Union have not yet materialised,' Flynn stresses. 'On the other hand, migratory pressures from the South, particularly from North Africa, have increased for both demographic and economic reasons.'

The new report focuses on three key components of an effective immigration policy:

* reduction of migration pressure through cooperation with the main countries of would-be emigration to Europe. Flynn says this will

involve action at a number of different levels such as trade, development aid and humanitarian assistance;

* better control of immigration through 'common approaches' to admission policies for workers, students and refugees. Preventive measures for combating illegal immigration and employment are also recommended. 'The focus for the purpose of asylum policies should be on ensuring that the examination for applications can continue to operate in a fair and efficient manner,' Flynn says;

* stronger efforts to integrate legal immigrants. Third country nationals in the Union should be treated no differently from EU citizens.

These broad aims form part of a 32-point action programme to turn piecemeal and unenforceable agreements among ministers into a comprehensive EU policy on immigration. 'We want to stimulate debate and discussion,' an aide to Flynn emphasises. 'The message is let's be tough on illegal immigrants, but tender with foreigners who are legally resident here.' The debate on Flynn's paper is just beginning.'

MARIA ECONOMOU/CAMERA PRESS

Albanian refugee 1991: Kicked out and boxed in

ISABELLE LIGNER

Towards year zero

'The new immigration laws put us in an impossible situation, our hands are tied', a weary magistrate in the huge hall of Nanterre's law court complains. Stringent new legislation leaves her little room for manoeuvre and she has just been forced to return three would-be immigrants to their country of origin.

Yet France's interior minister, Charles Pasqua, has been accusing the nation's magistrates of failing to follow the spirit of his reforms. His anger was triggered by the ruling of a Lyons judge reversing the decision of the local prefect to deport two young Algerians on 24 March 1994. While French participants were allowed to return home, Mouloud Madaci and Abdelkakim Youki were arrested and summarily deported for throwing stones during a demonstration against the government. Following the judicial decision, they were reunited with their families in France.

Since the minister had hoped this particular case would vindicate his 'zero immigration' policy, he was provoked into lashing out against the judges. 'The job of magistrates' he announced in April, 'is to implement laws not make them.'

Using a loophole in the law, a growing number of magistrates, particularly in Paris, are demonstrating their opposition to the heavy-handed treatment of France's 3.6 million immigrants (6.4% of the population) by releasing immigrants who have been notified of their deportation by administrative authorities. 'A law cannot prevent us from setting someone free', Alain Vogelweit of the Magistrates' Trade Union claims. 'Constitutionally speaking, a judge is the guarantor of freedom'.

But these guardians of freedom are finding it hard to hold the line against the arsenal of repressive measures enacted by the new law.

Immigration has been the first, and so far only, major area of reform under Edouard Balladur's right-wing (RPR) government since its election in March 1993. In place of the old revolutionary slogan, liberty, equality, fraternity, France has been presented with a new trilogy — nationality, identity, residence.

Children born in France of non-French parents have lost the automatic right to French nationality, and foreigners married to a French national must now wait two years before acquiring membership of the increasingly exclusive club of French citizens.

The new law has also introduced random identity checks, 'not according to racial criteria', the Act reads, 'but on an appraisal of the individual's general behaviour'. In practise, however, the law has been used to discriminate against the visibly different and has resulted in several suicides by illegal immigrants fearing discovery and deportation.

The most far-reaching changes cover the right of residence. In August 1993, the Constitutional Council rejected this section of the act on the grounds that it breached the French constitution. The final draft, enacted on 19 November after a change in the constitution, strengthens the 'struggle against illegal immigrants' and makes provision for their immediate deportation, a measure known in the ministry as 'escorting to the border'. Deportees can also be forbidden to

return for several years. Local mayors who conduct civil weddings, now have the power to prevent a wedding should they consider either party is going through the ceremony simply to obtain French nationality.

In conclusion, the law subjects the right of asylum to the same logic: reducing immigration flows to point zero. In conformity with other members of the European Union under the terms of the Schengen agreement, France also denies entry to asylum seekers if they have already been refused in any other member of the EU.

Along with Austria, France's record on political asylum is the worst in Western Europe. 'France used to be a country where everyone was welcome, this is not what the French want anymore,' asserts the Interior Minister. 'It is one more insult to the children of the workforce France courted in the 1960s', says Samira, a 19-year-old student whose father was recruited by a French industrialist in a Moroccan village 30 years ago. Foreigners, particularly those from the Mahgreb, have become scapegoats for all the problems afflicting French society, from upheavals in the suburbs and unemployment to Islamic fundamentalism and the failure of the education system.

Pasqua's philosophy is particularly hard on refugees from former-Yugoslavia and Algeria. Following an attempt to rationalise Ofpra (*Office Francais de protection des refugies et apatrides*), the number of asylum seekers fell dramatically from 60,000 in 1989 to 25,000 in 1992. Of the 500,000 ex-Yugoslavs seeking asylum in the EU only 1,000-2,000 were granted the right to stay in France and many were threatened with deportation.

The official attitude to potential Algerian immigrants is even tougher. 'If the fundamentalists took power in Algeria, we would not be in a position to accept any refugees in France,' said Pasqua earlier this month. As the killings mount on the other side of the Mediterranean, a civil servant in the Nanterre prefecture, Pasqua's own constituency, confides quietly that the French owe nothing to the Algerians, adding that it is 'their turn to be faced with the alternative they offered us (during the Algerian war of independence): the suitcase or the coffin'.

On 16 May, Abou B, an 18-year old delinquent who had just been released from prison was deported to Algeria, a country he left at the age of three and where he has no family. He speaks no Arabic and has little notion of Islam, a poor guarantee of safety in present day Oran. He was forbidden to return for five years and, given his criminal record, has no right of appeal.

Immigrants suffering from terminal illnesses such as cancer or Aids are shown no mercy. Alberto, an HIV positive Colombian following a course of treatment, was put on a plane in January. He has since returned to France clandestinely.

His case illustrates the futility of attempting to implement draconian immigration laws. Unless pursued with the rigour of a police state, their only apparent result is an increase in the number of illegal immigrants.

But pressure on the illegals also sends messages to legal immigrants: 'We tolerate you but you are not welcome'. 'We must maintain pressure on them,' a representative repeated fanatically as he left the court in Nanterre.

MIKHAIL X

Letter from Oranienburg

Introduction by Milen Radev

I met Mikhail for the first time almost a year ago when the authorities in
Berlin asked me to translate his letter home. What was their prisoner
writing to his brother in that small Bulgarian village? To me he was just
another Bulgarian Turk trying to get a foothold in Germany who
collided with the law in an unknown country, partly as a result of his
own negligence and partly because of a total lack of understanding of the
complex relationships in a different society.

He was a man in his 30s, who recalled the brutality of the Communist
name-changing campaign in Bulgaria in 1985. After the first shock,
hundreds of thousands of ethnic Turks fled to Turkey; a couple of years
later, most of them came back, especially after the downfall of the regime
in Sofia and the restoration of their rights. Mikhail had been in Turkey
also, but only for a short time and had returned quite disillusioned about
the prospects of finding a job there.

One year before I met him, his wife had left the village unexpectedly
for Germany and had found something of a job in a Turkish bar in West
Berlin. She had left Mikhail alone with their four children, aged between
12 and two.

Like thousands of his compatriots, Mikhail became unemployed. At
his wit's end he sold the house, took the children and, travelling via
Romania and Poland, reached the German border at the River Elbe
which they forded on foot at night.

He applied for political asylum and met his wife. She agreed to take
over the children and divorce him; he was to pay her half the money

from the house sale. With the rest he bought a car which he could resell later in Bulgaria for a handsome profit. However, as the letter recounts, he was arrested and charged with larceny.

When I met him, Mikhail had spent over a month in detention without any interrogation other than the initial questioning at the police station. He had not seen a solicitor and had no idea how to demand one. In comparable cases local citizens await their judicial hearing out on bail. As an asylum seeker he was assumed to have no permanent address and liable to flee. It seemed that the only alternative was detention in custody for an indefinite period. Mikhail was transferred to another prison soon after our meeting and I lost track of him.

Mikhail's letter was written in laboured Bulgarian. Most Turkish was not taught in Bulgarian schools, only Bulgarian, and Russian. For most, Turkish remains the spoken language but they are unable to write it.

20 April 1993

Dear Brother!

Today I felt sad for you, so I decided to sit down and write a few strokes and send you a letter. Brother, I sorrow without you a great deal and I keep dreaming of you. I just want to come back, I am sick and tired of this Germany. Seven months have passed away since I left Bulgaria. Brother, let me first of all ask, how are you, do you have any job, is there work to be found, how are the children, do they go to school, how is *bulya* [sister in law], does she work anywhere?

How is brother Ismet, does he feel good, is he going to work, is he still employed at the road-construction office, does *bulya* Emine go to work, are the children of brother Ismet in good health, do they still behave fine, have you had any letters from sister Fatme in Turkey?

Brother, how is doing Sevdjan, is my poor sister still a lodger, without a roof over her head like myself? But I promise, when I make a little money, please God, I will buy a flat and will take Sevdjan with the brother-in-law to stay with me, no more living in strange farmyards, how is Sevdjan's child, growing up the little fatty, I suppose?

What about Aleytin, sure, he must be in the army by now. Do you visit mother, how does she feel, I know that all the work is resting with her as ever, she is sweating and straining like the slave Isaura [character in a Brazilian soap-opera, shown on Bulgarian TV]. Brother, do look her up as often as you can, when you are not busy. When I still lived at home, I looked her up — every third day I dropped in on mother's. Brother, without me living near by, mother feels lonely and feeble, who shall protect her now that Aleytin is far away also, so she is certainly lonely. You are the only one, brother, left for her, please look her up from time to time so as to avoid her feeling lonesome until I return home.

But enough about concerns, let me write about my situation here, I know that you are interested how I get along in Germany. It could be worse — just after arriving in Germany I became asylum *(sic)* — that means I am an immigrant now. I live in a village called Wassmannsdorf near Berlin which is the capital here, not more than 30km away. We are sleeping in a sort of building, like a hostel. Brother, almost every day I visit Berlin I have a free monthly season ticket for the U-Bahn, that means underground railway, and they pay me every month DM400 also.

MILEN RADEV

The little ones are here in Berlin, they live together with my slut in a nice flat, the children are all right. Every other day I go and take them for a walk through Berlin, all four of them. I am so glad that I got rid of her, she will stay in Berlin for good, I don't have to bother about her any more. It's only living without the children that breaks my heart, but when they grow up, they will find me, I am sure. Little Metin keeps saying Father, this Germany is very boring, I don't understand German and I don't have any friends here.

Dear brother, let me tell you what a big misfortune came upon me.

All the money I possessed was DM4700. I found a good car for Bulgaria and bought it for DM4500, it was a splendid, brand new Lada Forma. This was all the money I had, but it happened that a police patrol stopped me to check all the documents and as they had a close look at everything, they became suspicious and put all the papers into the computer and then the car proved to be stolen. I had not the slightest notion that the car could be stolen but now I am arrested as the documents of the car were found to be fakes, as well as the registration number. For more than a month I have been locked up, I am just sitting in jail in a small town called Oranienburg. I have no idea what will happen further to me, they told me that the case is under investigation and that I am suspected of being the thief.

Dear brother, what should I write you more about myself? I have only bad luck in life — my family broke asunder, I lost my house and finally to make things even worse all my money is gone. Brother, do not tell mother that I am jailed, lest she will be worried about me, best of all, do not mention having a letter from me, because she will surely insist on reading my letter. When I am released from prison, I will try to get a labour permit from the big chief of the social office, we are entitled to work for 3 or 4 hours a day. It is only the chief of the social office who can make the decision. So I will try at last to regain a part of my great loss. The devil takes this car, I do not need a car any more, I am going to save a little money if I can.

That will be enough from me for today, do not worry about me, everything will turn good, you will see, it was just my fate to suffer.

My love to all of you.

Mikhail

Dear brother, do not answer my letter, maybe soon I shall be transferred to another prison, when I get released, I shall phone you. Dear brother, I forgot to ask you, do you still keep drinking? Please, stop that drinking, look how expensive life is, the children are growing, there is not work anywhere. Excuse me for being so daring! Goodbye, I wish you good health and success in life.

LESZEK SZARUGA

Post-German, post-Jewish

DMITRY PEISAKHOV/CAMERA PRESS

Borders are lines we see on maps, or checkpoints we cross when we travel by land. Our ancestors travelled by land, but borders meant less and national distinctions did not always provoke war

'Post-German' was the term we used for everything the Germans had left behind: furniture, books, houses, streets. My childhood was full of it. I lived in a small village called Glebokie near Szczecin. A walk to the woods could yield a whole range of fascinating objects: mines, guns, pistols, grenades. They were my childhood toys. And it's extraordinary that in all the time we used them in our games, we incurred the loss of only a single arm.

My parents collected post-German artefacts: a 40-volume collection of the complete works of Goethe rescued from a peasant household just as it was about to be used for fuel; a Steinway grand serving as a bar-counter which the barman used to slide beer mugs to his guests; some nice modernist furniture which had somehow survived the war. It was all post-German.

My parents were 'pioneers'; this was what the official press called the inhabitants of the new western territories assigned to Poland. In official parlance they were the 'recovered lands', but the settlers called them the 'western wilds'. Most of the pioneers travelled or were deported here from *Kresy,* the lost territories of eastern Poland, lands east of the river Bug, reaching as far as the river Neman to the north and the river Dniester to the south. People of many different nationalities lived here: Ukrainians, Lithuanians, Belorussians, Russians, Poles, Jews, Germans, Hungarians, Romanian, Czechs and French. In Polish literature the region had been dubbed *Miedzymorze* or 'The Land between the Seas': the Baltic and the Black Sea. After World War II it ceased to exist.

Jerzy Stempowski once wrote: 'All these shades of nationality and language were in a semi-fluid state. Frequently, the sons of Poles were called Ukrainians, the sons of Germans and Frenchmen — Poles. In Odessa Greeks became Russians; Poles joined the 'Union of the Russian People'. Mixed marriages led to even greater ethnic complexities... Nationality was not a racial issue, there was no inevitability about it. It was largely a matter of choice. And the choice was not limited to language. In the Dniester valley, which bore the vestiges of so many great civilisations, every language carried different historical, religious and social traditions, each had a specific ethical system, developed by centuries of triumph and disaster, aspiration and debate.'

Reading this, I understood why my own father, who was born in Odessa, felt that it was equally important that his lineage was Lithuanian and that his mother was Greek. At home they spoke Russian, though the language was neither my grandfather's nor my grandmother's. After leaving the Soviet Union, the family settled in Gdynia. My father was of mixed parentage, which made him a Pole. After almost five years imprisonment in a German POW camp, he came to Szczecin with his new Kaszub bride from Gdansk. They both spoke excellent German and later translated German literature, including Thomas Mann's *Doctor Faustus*. They were cast ashore in Szczecin by political circumstance. Nor were they alone. It was here that people with 'inconvenient' pasts found refuge, those who were seeking to cover their tracks. But above all, this was the place designated for the people who had lost their homelands beyond the Bug. Where were they to go?

Official propaganda did everything to confirm their sense of mission to settle these 'eternally Polish lands'. They, however, knew perfectly well that here even the stones cried out in German. They could see the gravestones, the Church inscriptions...

Years on I would reach for a historical atlas, leaf through its pages, and look upon the ever changing borders of the Polish state. Once it had lain on the river Oder, then it moved away, now it was back. I saw in this not a restoration, but a reparation. I thought about it in terms of the cost of the war Germany had lost. If she had won, Poland would doubtless not

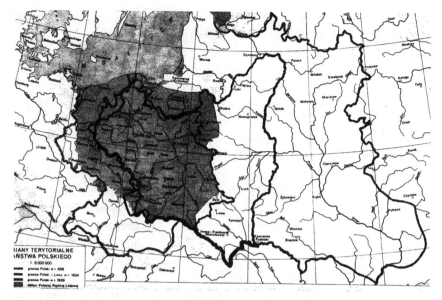

Historical atlas 1967: mutating borders, misplaced people

exist, and the German border would be in the Kamchatka. But she had lost. Historical arguments were unimportant. This is what they deserved, I thought. Post-German life left me indifferent. But this was not true of my friends and colleagues. To them, post-German meant alien, unwanted. Their homes were nourished by a different sense of space and other landscapes. When I visited them I would see mementos of Wilno or Lwow. They, and their parents, spoke a strange, melodious kind of tongue. It wasn't the Polish we spoke at home.

Gradually, I came to understand that for these people, and especially for their parents, settling in Szczecin was a punishment for crimes they didn't understand and had never committed. They had been uprooted and sent into an alien, hostile environment. There was nothing of the victor or pioneer about them. On the contrary, they were longing for a home they had lost. The more so since they could neither speak nor write about it. 'Their eyes spoke of the fear and confusion of people herded out into the unknown', Katarzyna Sucholska writes in her story 'A meeting in Wolkenberg'. Attempts were made to rob them, to destroy the memory of generations. They spent decades sitting on suitcases, waiting for a miracle to happen. In their flats, beside other mementos of their lost home, they kept little bags of earth.

In 1968 a brutal anti-Semitic campaign was unleashed in Poland and many people were forced to leave the country. Frequently their only connection with Judaism lay in a dim and distant past. Friends told me with a mixture of surprise and fear that they had only just learned of their Jewish background. Many were categorised as Jews because they were 'outlanders'. Though the police generally checked, I too was exposed to arrest and insult, but received an official apology in prison a few days later. That was how I discovered that the police held dossiers relating to the background and nationality of Polish citizens. Perhaps it is true that someone, somewhere, always collects documents of this kind.

The anti-Semitic campaign launched by the Communists took place in an atmosphere of social acquiescence, much like the German extermination of the Jews in Poland in the 1940s. The two events bear no comparison, of course. Just as one cannot conclude from them that Poles are anti-Semites by nature. They are as anti-Semitic as the French or the Germans: they display xenophobia when the conditions are right. Clearly, not everyone is actively involved. Not even the majority. But a minority can dominate the rest, and the majority be helpless in the face of rampant evil.

I remember my own helplessness and despair; and the guilt which remains with me even now. I remember a long walk around the streets of Warsaw with the distinguished Polish poet Arnold Slucki. He had been born into a Jewish family in the early 1920s and joined the Communist Party as a boy. He came from a small village, in what is now Ukraine. Slucki knew no Polish then, only Ukrainian and Yiddish. Later, he learned other languages. He spent the war in the Soviet Union, and then chose to live in Poland. He learned the language, began to write and became a distinguished lyric poet. He told me all this because he had to tell someone who was staying and whom he could trust. He was leaving the following day. He went via Vienna to Israel, but longed to return. He moved back to Europe and as close to Warsaw as he could, settling in West Berlin. More than 20 years ago he was buried in the Ruhleben cemetery. He was barely 50. That is how exiles and those who have been hounded out of their homes come to die: silent, unnoticable deaths.

I remember seeing my friends off on that train to Vienna. And those repeated farewells when the exiles distributed possessions they would not or could not take with them: books, furniture, paintings, household utensils. Nor will I ever forget learning a new word that day. It was the adjective 'post-Jewish', and meant everything the Jews had left behind...

We live in this nightmare daily. At times its manifestations are more intense, at times less so. To resist it we must first give it a name. We have called it racism, nationalism, xenophobia, enmity towards strangers, but today words like this mean little. In recent decades the phenomenon has undergone changes which are hard to express. And although we frequently make analogies between this new wave of hostility to outsiders and the inter-war years, I feel that this tends to obscure rather than clarify the real state of things.

The explosion of nationalisms before World War II came when the idea of the 'nation state' was at the height of its popularity. The present debacle is an expression of the same idea in crisis. One of its causes is undoubtedly the lack of any alternative political concept that is widely accepted or understood. Perhaps it is a question of finding a new educational approach. The model which has nurtured us and which recounts the history of nations has proved deceptive. Can we find a substitute? Not so long ago national distinctions did not, of necessity, provoke tensions. Wars were fought to settle conflicts of a different kind. Rulers changed, but this did not mean that the inhabitants of their lands were driven out.

One answer might lie in the return to a cultural perspective lost in recent decades. In the 18th century, it gave every educated European a sense of belonging to a community which shared an idiom descended from a common Greek and Roman antiquity, a familiarity with the classic texts, and a sense of European cultural identity alive in Athens, Sofia, Constantinople, Rome, Paris, Lisbon, Oslo, Stockholm, London or Vienna. Borders are lines we see on maps, or check-points we cross when we travel by land. Our ancestors travelled by land more than we do, but borders meant less to them...

Translated by Irena Maryniak

Willkommen, bienvenue, welcome...

MILEN RADEV

VÁCLAV HAVEL

Out of unity, discord

'If we are too careful, slow, hesitant and reserved, the new order could be built by others, in particular the nationalists and chauvinists'

(Left) Bosnia 1992: betrayed by Europe:
Billie Rafaeli/Camera Press
(Above) Credit: Oldrich Skacha

Czechoslovakian border 1989: on the road to a new European order

The writer-President of the Czech Republic is no stranger to controversy. As the leading dissident in Communist Czechoslovakia, he was imprisoned, internally exiled and under constant surveillance for his outspoken criticism of the regime. Now, as master in his own land, he is equally forthright — and uncompromising — on those issues exercising post-Communist Europe. Here he talks to Igor Blazevic, of the Helsinki Citizens' Assembly, about the European peace initiatives in Bosnia and the urgency of finding ways of 'co-existence' between nations and communities in the post-Communist world.

Mr President, you have repeatedly called on the international community to adopt a firmer position on Bosnia. Given that raising your voice was politically risky, why did you do it?

There are three reasons why I spoke out. I am firmly convinced that in today's world of multiple inter-connections, it is possible systematically to strengthen and spread a sense of common responsibility. This means that we are all actually responsible for the whole world, not just for violent conflicts but for the environment and for a number of other spheres. The current world of politics lacks this feeling of global responsibility. This is the philosophical-political reason.

A more concrete reason is that historically the Czech Republic's record on democracy is not good; it has not shown much capacity for engaging in democracy even though our own values — and the ones on which the Republic is founded — are those of democracy. We discovered this most clearly at Munich. At the time (1938), after the Munich agreement, [UK Prime Minister] Chamberlain said that he could not understand why an Englishman should risk his life for a country about which he knows little. We know the consequences of this. This hope — that in the name of peace one must sacrifice values to protect human lives — was shown to be an utter illusion. The effect was precisely the opposite. No lives were saved. In the end many more were sacrificed. When the international community's hesitation to get involved in the situation in Bosnia-Hercegovina and in the whole of former Yugoslavia can once again have self-destructive consequences, particularly for Europe, this analogy commands our attention. The unification of Europe is based on co-existence, the co-existence of various nations, cultures and religions. When they are in such close proximity, in a space which is part of the political reality of Europe, and when those values are being contested, trampled on and brutally mocked in the name of neo-nationalism and ethnic cleansing, then it is directly endangering the values on which Europe alone stands and on which it is uniting. It is not merely a question of solidarity with suffering, but of solidarity for our own sake; not allowing such hesitations to endanger the principles of our own lives.

The final reason has, maybe, more to do with my own nature: I am angered by indifference to violence and injustice.

However, when I do, from time to time, raise my voice, I am always a little uneasy. I am not someone who can boldly enter the issue, far less someone who will risk his life. And I am uneasy because it is not I who am making the decisions but the international community — the North Atlantic Alliance, the European Union, the United Nations. It is a little odd when someone who does not personally bear the consequences of a decision, advises others. Of course, if we imagine some kind of greater international action, where various states could be called on to participate, then we can imagine Czech units participating in some form. Nevertheless, it is easier for someone who is not directly deciding to advise than it is for someone who carries the consequences of that decision.

But in spite of my uneasiness, I have, for a long time now, stressed at various international events, that Bosnia is more than a local skirmish; that it is a question of elementary values on which not only European unity depends but on which the co-existence of people around the world could also depend. One of the greatest dangers to the world's growing

11 November 1989: the night the Wall came down

population is precisely the conflict between nations or communities that is based purely on their sense of difference from one another. It could be the gravest threat to today's world.

You have criticised the Geneva negotiations. In a joint statement with Slovene President Milan Kucan, you said that the international community needs to re-define its political goal in Bosnia. Is this still necessary and is it still capable of doing so?

During the Geneva negotiations I became increasingly uneasy. I was most disturbed when I got the impression that various wild fighters were conquering various territories and drawing various maps which the Geneva Conference accepted, adopted, completed and looked for maps of ethnic divisions which would accommodate the three warring sides. This seems to me a typical example of forsaking the defence of values around which our existence revolves. It gave me the impression that Karadzic more or less offered the Geneva negotiators themes for their negotiations. I was not only sceptical, I felt there was a certain hypocrisy. Because they didn't want to admit that the negotiations were deadlocked, they carried on, on the logical and highly plausible grounds that it is essential to get the warring parties round a negotiating table as a peaceful means of securing a truce that may, in the end, lead to peace.

However, in reality these negotiations agreed to something that is essentially alien to the institutions involved. You cannot change borders and divide states by force and expect them to remain internationally recognised. Nor can you simultaneously continue to recognise existing borders and rush into negotiations with wild armed forces on how a state will be changed into several different states.

But it seems that the situation has changed somewhat since then. The idea of a Muslim-Croat federation in some kind of confederal relation with Croatia, seems to be acceptable to its citizens. If it succeeds, and I have serious doubts, in finally linking Bosnian Serbs to the federation, and in being recognised, and in rebuilding on the federal principle, it could be a possible solution.

We ourselves have experienced this: we were two nations, each of whom felt independent and expressed this independence in constitutional terms. We strove to construct a just federation which, as everyone knows, failed. So we finally agreed to part peacefully. I am not so naive that I cannot understand the need nations feel to have their own state. But what bothers me in Bosnia-Hercegovina is that the communities there are interwoven and related; the network of co-existence was rich. Such a division on ethnic principles might never end. A border could run through every home, every family, every village. Speculation would be never-ending to the point of absurdity.

A couple of years ago it seemed that with the end of Communism and the Cold War, we were moving towards a better Europe. But few now speak about the end of history, the new world order and grand European integration. They speak instead about the division of civilisations whose boundaries will run through European soil. Western Europe is more and more resembling a castle which defends only itself and is indifferent to those who are rebuilding. If you think the European democracies are failing, then why is that? What kind of dangers are still before us? What could be done to prevent Europe looking worse than it does today?

You are right about the atmosphere of general enthusiasm in the first months of 1990 following the fall of the Iron Curtain. We imagined Europe would move towards a new order more quickly and more easily than it actually has. But this doesn't mean we are not living in the creative phase of the new order. It is being created and must emerge, but the road to this order is far more painful and complicated than first seemed.

However, with resolution, creativity and courage we can search for and build this new order. Traditional politics, guided by pragmatism and caution, are not enough; we have to go beyond stereotypes. There are successful examples of traditional politics being transcended. Remember the period after World War II: a generation of courageous politicians like de Gaulle, Adenauer, Churchill and others who, after the experiences of World War II and with the painful experience of Stalin's designs on Europe, succeeded, at least in Western Europe, in constructing a new and better order. The century of German-French confrontation ended and the unification process began. The search for a new order demands that today's politicians have the same courage and generosity as those of earlier generations. If they are too careful, slow, hesitant and reserved, the new order could be built by others, in particular by various nationalists and chauvinists.

People in Bosnia-Hercegovina, who were in favour of democracy and a multi-ethnic state, feel defeated by nationalism and fascism and betrayed by Western democracy.

I absolutely know and understand this feeling. In addition to the three warring sides there is a powerful fourth side that does not want war and does not feel the need for confrontation between different ethnic groups. I am on their side. At the same time, whenever we say someone betrayed us, or we are angry with someone, we must examine our own position. In one way or another, the leaders of the current conflict were chosen: Karadzic was elected as the representative of a certain party in the elections in Bosnia-Hercegovina. This society must reflect on its own errors or failures, not simply place the entire responsibility on others.

When you speak about Bosnia do you feel any conflict between Havel the intellectual and Havel the politician?

I confess this problem is perhaps more distressing for some commentators than for myself. I don't feel it's such a big problem. Fate put me in a role where I have to express views in a way fitting to my function as president. I'd have done the same even if I were not president, I simply have to choose different words, maybe more diplomatic or more careful, but I must remain myself and say what I really think. I take it simply as a new challenge, a job that has to be done and with which I must somehow cope. It's nothing new: throughout my life fate has faced me with various strange tasks; perhaps it was their odd and unusual nature that challenged me, provoked me into doing something.

Prague 1990: The President and the T-shirt.
'If Samuel Beckett had been born in
Czechoslovakia, we'd still be waiting for Godot'
(see p190 Obituary)

ANTONIN NOVY/AP

MIINORITIES: ROMANI

DONALD KENRICK

On the move once more

T GOULDEN

According to Andrzej Mirga, president of the Roma Association of Poland, Romani [also known as gypsies] occupy the lowest and most stigmatised social position in the former Soviet Bloc states. He told the US Congress in April that although the totalitarian and centralised systems conducted assimilationist policies aimed at erasing Romani identity, they were at least guaranteed work, health care, education and housing, and were also protected from open discrimination and violence. But now, after many centuries of settled life, the turbulence in the new states of eastern Europe is forcing the Romani onto the move again.

For the approximately four million Romani living in eastern Europe, the fall of Communism has had both negative and positive consequences. On the positive side, there is greater freedom to travel, to set up organisations — including political parties — and to publish their own newspapers and magazines. On the negative side, racist propaganda is flourishing and racist violence is tolerated. Furthermore, the move to capitalist economies has meant the shedding of unskilled labour and Romani are often the first to be dismissed.

Anti-Romani racism is rife throughout eastern Europe. In Bulgaria, there has long been a popular mistrust of its minorities under the surface of an apparently tolerant society. With press freedom, prejudice came into the open and scaremongering headlines such as the following appeared: 'Turks rape, Gypsies rob in the middle of Sofia'; 'Gypsies chase doctors with knives'; 'Gypsies steal Easter eggs from churchyard'.

Although the Romani population in Poland is comparatively small — numbering around 50,000 people — the majority population is hostile. Here, as elsewhere, the Romani have replaced the Jews as the scapegoats for economic problems. Wall posters read 'Death to the Romani' and 'Hang the Romani'. The *Narodowy Front Polski* (National Front) has circulated anti-Romani leaflets: 'They [the Romani] are a very disgusting and painful abscess on the body of our Nation....Let them pack their dirty tatters and leave Poland for ever.'

During the Ceausescu dictatorship in Romania, Romani were the object of discrimination by all the authorities. However, they are now the focus of a popular racism to which right-wing and centre political parties pander. *Romania Mare*, a popular weekly magazine, demanded the expulsion of all Romani as early as 1991. *Vatra Romanesca*, an ultra-nationalist political movement which claims 400,000 sympathisers, announced that the 'holy ground of Romania has been spoiled by the feet of Asiatics, Huns, Romani and other vagabonds.' A rumour that the despised Ceausescu was himself Romani is common currency.

In Slovakia the Prime Minister, Vladimir Meciar, has referred to Romani as 'a great burden on society' and suggested that their social security payments should be cut to stop them having children.

Racist violence against Romani in eastern Europe is reminiscent of pogroms against the Jews in the Tsarist Empire. In the Czech Republic attacks have steadily increased and 21 Romani have been killed. Last year 300 people marched through the town of Pardubice with baseball bats shouting 'Romani to the gas chambers'. There is a self-imposed curfew in many towns, because Romani fear being attacked by skinheads. In Prague Romani are barred from popular bars and discotheques.

Attacks on Romani seem to follow a pattern: a quarrel between a Romani and a non-Romani sparks off a mass attack on Romani homes. On 16 October 1993, such a quarrel near the village of Cherganovo escalated from a fist fight between two Bulgarians and a Romani cowherd into a mob attack on the Romani quarter of the village. At the call of the church bells, a crowd of 60 Bulgarians armed with spades and axes ransacked five houses, smashing windows and doors and breaking furniture. In one home, four Romani adults and two children were beaten, and two other children were shot at. During the attack four policemen stood by doing nothing. Led by the mayor the Bulgarians then went to a bar to celebrate, after which they returned to the Romani quarter a second time. They set fire to hay, broke into a house and sat there drinking until morning. All the Romani fled from the village and sheltered with relatives in neighbouring areas. There have been 16 similar pogroms in Romania since 1991. The last was in 1993 in Hadareni where three Romani were killed and 10 homes were burnt.

The majority of Romani in the Czech Republic were previously settled in Slovakia but were encouraged to move west under Communism. However, many Czech towns tried, even before the establishment of the new republic, to bring in bye-laws to keep out Romani born in the eastern areas of old Czechoslovakia. A competitor for the crown of Miss Czech Republic 1993, Magdalena Babicka, achieved a brief moment of fame when she said her great ambition was to 'cleanse Czech cities of their dark-skinned inhabitants'. In Usti nad Labem, the home of Miss Babicka, 120 flats were raided by police in December 1992 looking for unregistered tenants from Slovakia. New national citizenship laws which came into force on 1 January 1993 make it harder for Romani to qualify for citizenship of the Czech Republic. If they or their parents were born in Slovakia they have to apply to become Czechs. Citizenship is granted only if applicants pass a language test, have had a permanent residence for two years and no convictions for five. The five-year period stretches back into the Communist era when crimes included offences that are no longer on the statute book, such as 'leading a parasitic life', defined as being self-employed or an being an unmarried woman living in her parents' home. The one Romani MP in the Czech Parliament, Ladislav Body, will have to apply for Czech citizenship or lose his home (and presumably his parliamentary seat). Romani born in the Czech Republic but refused citizenship are not automatically eligible for Slovak citizenship. Many will become stateless in the new Europe.

At least 250,000 Romani were killed in the Nazi period, many in the puppet states in the East. Attempts to rewrite history and deny this genocide are afoot. In several countries collaborators are being rehabilitated on the grounds that they were anti-Communist, not pro-fascist. On the eve of the 45th anniversary of his execution in 1946 for war crimes, the wartime dictator Marshal Antonescu was honoured with a minute's silence in the Romanian Parliament. It is said that he was not responsible for the death of Romani but tried to protect them. According to the new version of history, the reason he deported thousands of Romani to the occupied Ukraine where 36,000 died of hunger and brutal treatment was to save them from the camps in Germany.

The Hungarian historian László Karsai reduces the number of Hungarian Romani dead to 'a few hundred', compared to earlier figures of over 28,000: 'The concentration camps were not extermination camps and the members of the (Romani) families were not separated, indeed in most of the camps in Poland and Austria Romani prisoners were not even forced to work.' His book *The Gypsy Question in Hungary 1919-1945* makes no mention of the extermination centres at Treblinka and Chelmno, or any of the other camps where Romani were forced into hard labour and the survivors shot on the death marches.

The violence, allied to their poor economic situation, has made many Romani see migration west as the answer. So far it is only from Romania and Poland that a substantial percentage are actually leaving. Those with Polish citizenship tend to travel to the West as tourists and then apply for political asylum. The latest figure from British government sources showed that 160 heads of family made such an application at one point last year. None have been accepted. The attitude of Western governments is that what is happening in Poland is not 'persecution' but 'harassment', and therefore not covered by international conventions on refugees.

Romani from Romania fleeing to the West are numbered in thousands. They arrived openly until the German border posts stopped anyone who did not have a sponsor, so now they come illegally. It is estimated that some 40,000 Romanian Romani have come to Germany and other Western countries. Germany has started mass repatriation of asylum seekers and has promised the Romanian government over US$15 million to set up training centres for returning refugees. This follows a smaller scheme for repatriating Macedonian Romani.

Emigration may be the solution for some but for most the hope must be that social and economic conditions can be improved in the countries where they have lived for many generations, otherwise neither visa controls nor frontiers will stop a new migration of the Romani.

The Romani of Bulgaria and Romania

'No-one stands up for them. No state will take
them in. Because they are different, possessed of
that disturbing beauty which makes us look ugly...
deeply sad, desperately light hearted. They would
teach us how pointless frontiers are, for the
Romani know no frontiers.'

All photographs: T Goulden

HUMAN RIGHTS

CAROLINE MOOREHEAD

A dangerous profession

Just over a year ago Ugur Mumcu, a much-respected columnist on the Turkish daily paper *Cumhuriyet*, was blown up as he was getting into his car in front of his house in Ankara. He had been working on an article about the Turkish secret services.

Last summer 19-year-old Ferhat Tepe, a reporter working in Bitlis, was leaving his father's shop when a man carrying a walkie-talkie ordered him into a car. Ferhat's bruised body was found by a fisherman in a near-by lake on 5 August.

Two days late, another young journalist, 22-year-old Aysel Malkac, who was seven months pregnant, vanished after leaving her office in Istanbul. Nothing has been heard of her since. And in the last two months, two more people connected with the same newspaper have disappeared: Nazim Babaoglu, who has been missing from his home in Urfa since 12 March, and Serif Avsar, the father of two small children, who was taken away from his office on 22 April. His body turned up on 7 May with two shots in the head. These deaths and disappearances of journalists are part of a pattern of human rights violations rapidly turning Turkey into one of the most violent countries in the world, where the government is either refusing or failing to bring the culprits to justice, and where the state security prosecutor in Ankara, Nusret Demiral, is renowned for the vigour of his campaigns against Turkey's 'enemies'.

Investigative journalism in Turkey today demands great bravery: investigations into the police, the army, business corruption, drugs, Islamic fundamentalism all put journalists at risk. Death threats are regularly followed by abduction and murder. Their courage, however, follows an honourable tradition. In 1971, writer Abdi Ipekci was shot dead in Istanbul when investigating a political story, while throughout the 1980s, in the wake of the military coup, editors and journalists regularly went to prison for their supposed Communist sympathies, most of them for 20 or even 30 years.

Ferhat Tepe, Aysel Malkac, Nazim Babaoglu and Serif Avsar were all linked to the Turkish-language, Kurdish-owned paper, *Özgür Gündem*, which has never made any secret of its support for the Kurdish Workers' Party, the PKK, who are engaged in civil war against the government and the military in Turkey's south-eastern provinces over the question of a separate Kurdish state. And *Özgür Gündem* has been the hardest hit of all liberal Turkish newspapers. Since beginning publication in May 1992, six of its journalists and 12 others connected with it, have been killed; over 250 of its people have been arrested, held, and many of them tortured; and its issues are repeatedly confiscated. Last year, 119 trials were opened against it, while 110 of its staff were detained during a police raid on 10 December, Human Rights Day, in Istanbul. Thirty-four of them are currently in detention, most still awaiting trial. At a time of unprecedented attacks on the media throughout the world, the story of *Özgür Gündem* and its battles with the Turkish state remains among the worst.

FROM CENT PHOTOS POUR LA LIBERTÉ DE LA PRESSE, RSF 1994

2 April 1993: daughters of a policeman, killed by an extreme left group, mourning their father

What is happening to Turkish journalists in 1994 has to be seen in the context of the country's political upheavals. In 1983, the government launched a campaign in south-east Turkey against those of the estimated 10 million Kurdish minority who were calling for a separate state. The following year, the PKK hit back with a first, violent, raid on a police post, in which a number of soldiers died. Since then, skirmishes and isolated incidents have turned into a civil war which has claimed, it is said, at least 12,000 dead, most of them civilians. When a new coalition government came to power in 1991, it promised to curb the increasingly brutal abuses of human rights throughout the south-east, most perpetrated by apparently unidentified death squads. The violence continued, and to this day 13 provinces remain under emergency regulations.

The torture of detainees, a phenomenon that plagued Turkey under the military rulers during the 1980s, is now once again on the increase: there were 23 deaths in detention last year. Their bodies showed signs of beating, rape, dog bites, gun wounds and electric shocks. Some had finger and toe nails missing. A woman lawyer and member of the Turkish Human Rights Association called Meral Danis Bestas has reported being slapped, kicked, stripped, hosed with freezing water, and sexually insulted during interrogation. Turkey has ratified both the United Nations and the European Conventions against torture.

Earlier this year, Tansu Ciller, the Prime Minister, (who has taken Lady Thatcher's suggestion to use the services of Saatchi and Saatchi to boost Turkey's image) vowed to crush the PKK in time for the March local elections, and to restore some kind of peace to the south-east. No such peace occurred and the continuing violence served only to drive more voters into supporting extreme right-wing parties.

But now the winter is over, the mountain passes are once again open, and a new spring offensive, believed to involve between 200,000 and 300,000 forces — some of them Special Teams trained in guerrilla warfare — has been launched. This time, the government has said, the war will end. Once again, the wholesale roundups of Kurdish villagers, the razing of villages suspected to support the PKK, disappearances and arbitrary executions are on the increase. There are rumours that the Turkish army has begun to use chemical weapons in the mountains near the Iraq-Iran border. Meanwhile, the PKK are responding in kind.

The Turks have long enjoyed a fairly uncensored press. Papers can print both articles and photographs of a scandalous kind. The private lives of politicians are not respected. But one subject remains absolutely taboo: that of the Kurds and their calls for independence. One of the country's best known comedians, Levent Kierca, has said that he intends to make fun of everyone and everything on his regular television shows but he will not mention anything at all to do with the Kurds.

Under the supposedly fairer Anti-Terror law that was introduced in April 1991 to replace some of the harsher articles of the Turkish Penal Code, a far tougher stand is being made against the print media. Articles 1, 6 and 8 effectively give the authorities powers to arrest, imprison and fine on charges so vague as to be almost meaningless. No violent act of any kind is necessary for a person to go to jail. One newspaper editor faces prison for failing to give his new address to the Istanbul authorities. In the last few months of 1993, dozens of issues of various papers were confiscated, books were banned, and hundreds of writers and reporters picked up. The editor-in-chief and some of the correspondents of the newspaper *Azadi* have been sentenced to more than 50 years in jail and fined huge sums, as have journalists on *Aydinlik, Newroz, Odak* and *Hedef.*

Not that the government's repressive attitude towards the Kurdish question is confined to journalists. Last month, Mehdi Zana, former mayor of Diyarbakir, centre of much of the trouble in the south-east, was sent to prison for four years for making 'separatist propaganda': he had spoken of the Kurdish conflict before the European Parliament in December 1992. In March, parliamentary immunity was lifted on five members of the Democracy Party (DEP) and one Independent. They now await trial for raising the Kurdish question. The charge carries a possible death sentence. And the editor of the *Turkish Daily News*, Izmet Imset, author of a balanced article on the Kurds, has decided not to return to Turkey from America, where, after accepting assurance that all his remarks would be confidential, he agreed to speak to Congress. But when an aide leaked his remarks to the Turkish authorities, Imset decided that returning would certainly mean prison, and possibly death.

If the government has taken an increasingly intransigent stand against journalists, the PKK cannot be said to have behaved very much better. In the last few months they have kidnapped two journalists, and halted the publication in the south-east of papers and magazines they decided were not giving them favourable enough coverage — though *Özgür Gündem*, to which their leader Abdullah Ocalan is said to contribute regular articles under different pseudonyms — was not among them. Death threats were made to the others to back up the order. Abdullah Ocalan is known to be a figure of considerable brutality. In his roots among the left-wing movements of the 1960s, and in his commitment to violence and use of terror to win villagers over to his cause, he is increasingly being compared to Pol Pot or Abimael Guzmán of Peru's *Sendero Luminoso*. In October, PKK guerrillas killed 35 prisoners, including two children, near Erzerum. In January, 16 women and children died when PKK men threw grenades into a building in which they had taken refuge. 'Censorship by the bullet', a ghastly phrase that has come to acquire real meaning in Turkey, is not confined to government forces.

Outside Turkey, the human rights world is extremely critical of the brutality of Turkey's army and government, which continues to insist that they have no idea about who is responsible for all the killing and disappearances other than 'terrorists'. It is appalled, too, by the way in which the UN human rights bodies seem unwilling to take a tough line; by the way that NATO continues to pour vast quantities of arms into the country — Turkey is said to have received 1,017 battle tanks last year, only seven less than the entire number of tanks in the British Army — and by the fact that Turkey, widely seen as strategically crucial to the West, continues to be inundated by grants to bolster its failing economy.

Pro-Kurdish journalists, eager to chronicle the Turkish govenment's brutality, are no less brave than others in the country. But there is something perhaps more tragic in their deaths, particularly those of *Özgür Gündem*'s workers, many of whom are dying in defence of an organisation whose methods are not only at least comparable in their brutality to those of the government forces, but are provoking the military and the authorities into ever more horrendous repression. But atrocious government violence does not prove its opponents righteous. Yet again, the losers can only be the ordinary Kurds. For them, trapped between the Turkish soldiers and the PKK, who are increasingly rejecting the democratic process, killed by one side or the other for their alleged sympathies, or simply caught in the cross fire, the future does not look bright.

RL/TIBET INFOMATION NETWORK

Tibet 1993: a glaring case of cultural genocide

CENTRE ON HOUSING
RIGHTS AND EVICTIONS

Demolition and reconstruction

'Should ... the 1980 Lhasa Development Plan be implemented in full,
Lhasa will have lost virtually all
Tibetan attributes by the turn of the
century and a further 10,000 Tibetans
will have been forcibly evicted from
their homes.' This startling claim is
made and examined in *Destruction by
Design: Housing Rights Violations in
Tibet*, published by the Centre on
Housing Rights and Evictions.

The Plan, which aims to demolish
virtually the entire centre of Lhasa,
the capital of Tibet, is perhaps the
most far-reaching of the occupying

Chinese government's policies in the
'Tibet Autonomous Region'. Using
'urban beautification' and the
improvement of infrastructure and
services as justification for the wide-
scale demolition of structurally-
sound Tibetan buildings, China is
transforming Lhasa inch-by-inch into
a Chinese city.

The main objective is the Barkhor, the old municipal area, which
will have all but disappeared by the
year 2000, save for a few temples,
monasteries and other buildings preserved for the sake of tourism. Plans
include the widening of streets,
ostensibly 'combining principles of
modern town planning with archi-
tectural grace', but, in practice, facil-
itating access by troops and police to
troublesome areas.

The Tibetan 'old city' of Lhasa
now occupies less than one square

kilometre, barely two per cent, of the total urban area. Shopping centres and concrete Chinese buildings in walled compounds are encroaching on the Barkhor. The city, which covers some 28 square kilometres, is dominated by such compounds which house police, army and government cadres brought in to enforce control, and thousands of economic migrants from China who are the main beneficiaries of housing and planning measures in Tibet.

The first book to deal explicitly with the issue of housing rights violations in Tibet, *Destruction by Design* provides an innovative and timely analysis of the sinocisation of Tibet. Focusing mainly on Lhasa, which has so far borne the brunt of China's 'reconstruction' policies, but is by no means the only city to suffer, the report uses maps, planning charts and photographs to show how the Chinese are moving in *en masse*, demolishing traditional Tibetan housing. Dozens of cases are cited, a fraction of the mass expulsions and evictions on racial grounds that have left thousands of Tibetans homeless or inadequately housed.

Using the case of Lhasa as a contemporary framework within which to explore the aims of international housing rights legislation, the report shows how occupying forces typically use housing and planning decisions as tools of social control, forcing minorities into cultural and economic ghettos. It calls on the Chinese government to redress the situation and bring housing law and policy into line with China's existing international legal obligations, and to provide Tibetans with the right to participate in and control their nation's development. But without a drastic and immediate reappraisal of current Chinese policy, the indigenous Tibetan population will become a tiny minority in itsown country, never again allowed the legitimate right to self-determination. *Annie Knibb*

Destruction by Design: Housing Rights Violations in Tibet (Centre on Housing Rights and Evictions, 199pp). Available from Centre on Housing Rights and Evictions, c/o Scott Leckie, Havikstraat 38 B/S, 3514 TR, Utrecht, The Netherlands

TSG MÜNICH

Lhasa 1994: forced reconstruction

HUMAN RIGHTS WATCH

Rough justice

Colombia, it has been said, is a country where life is so cheap, they're practically giving it away. The remark might be amusing were it not so close to the truth.

These Human Rights Watch reports show how thoroughly violence of all kinds, politically motivated or not, has permeated all sectors of society. Colombia's presidential human rights advisor refers to the ascending spiral of violence as a process of macabre democratisation: all become equal before the law of the gun.

Colombia is in the grip of the region's longest-running (albeit largely ignored) war, which would be bad enough without the added complication of US involvement in funding the putative war on drugs against the cocaine barons. Extensive shipments of helicopter gunships, jet aircraft, land mines, grenade launchers make Colombia the largest recipient of US military aid in Latin America.

And so the superlatives mount up: Colombia ranks third in the world for numbers of disappearances, and the rate of other human rights violations continues to soar.

Both the US and the Colombian governments hold the various insurgent groups accountable for the majority of abuses. Evidence uncovered by Human Rights Watch, however, contradicts this view. Even the US government's own General Accounting Office has more than once expressed concern over the lack of proper end-use monitoring for the aid supplied to the Colombian armed forces who themselves draw few distinctions between the drug threat and the guerrilla threat or between combatants and civilians.

Of course violations occur on both sides of the civil war. But just as worrying as the level of physical abuse is the level of administrative and judicial abuse to which the government has resorted. Under the rubric of a 'state of internal commotion', in late 1992 President Gaviria effectively halted the democratic opening that followed the adoption of the new Constitution in 1990. Rule by decree, curtailing of civil rights and unchecked brutality in the police and armed forces inevitably lead to the old systemic ills — corruption, arbitrariness, abuse — that have defined the region's politics for so long.

These ills are chiefly expressed through the symptom of impunity. When the state — through its agents, the armed forces — carries out massacres in rural villages, abductions, disappearances, arbitrary detentions, it is unrealistic, to say the least, for victims or their families to expect the state to provide justice or redress. It is ironic that members of the army's special UNASE unit, set up to prevent kidnapping and extortion by the military, have been found to be among the most enthusiastic exponents of those very practices.

One hundred and fifty UNASE

officers and soldiers have been arrested and are currently under investigation for extortion, but this is the exceptional case. Most perpetrators of abuse are simply left untouched by the law. Where none can be held properly accountable for their actions, the political process loses all pretence of justice and descends to the raw exercise of power. Whoever has the bigger weapons wins.

The individual's rights count for nothing under these conditions. In both Colombia and Brazil the most disquieting phenomenon known as 'social cleansing' has become commonplace. As with any euphemism, the term disguises the reality, rather than illuminating it. The reality is that this is violence against the weakest members of society. As the social fabric unravels, those at its fraying edges come to be seen as worthless and hence, in another repellent euphemism, 'disposable'; homosexuals, beggars, and the street children highlighted in the report on Brazil.

One notorious incident last July, in which off-duty police officers shot and killed eight children as they slept near Rio's Candelária church, focused international attention for a short time. But the Candelária massacre is only one spectacular instance of the problem and to focus too sharply on that alone only diminishes the routine nature of daily beatings, harassment and murders committed by police and private security forces.

Again, what the law says and what the law does are two different things. Brazil has some of the most progressive legislation for protecting

children's rights in the world. But in practice, Human Rights Watch finds official complicity in protecting the perpetrators of violence against children (with the notable exception of Candelária, for which four military policemen have been arrested) together with official denials that the problem even exists. In Brazil as in Colombia, it is that impunity, shrouded in silence, which creates the perfect climate for gross human rights violations to flourish.
Adam Newey

State of War: political violence and counterinsurgency in Colombia (December 1993, 149pp); *Final Justice: police and death squad homicides of adolescents in Brazil* (February 1994, 140pp), both Human Rights Watch/Americas. Fax: (212) 972 0905 (New York); (44) 71 713 1800 (London)

Taslima Nasreen, Bangladeshi writer, feminist and latest target of Islamic absolutism. Dr Nasreen has lived under the threat of execution since October last year when fundamentalist clerics in Bangladesh demanded her death. In June this year, following demands for her execution for blasphemy, President Khaleda Zia ordered her arrest. (Index Index p165)

HUMAN RIGHTS WATCH
announces

The 1994 Recipients
of the
Lillian Hellman/Dashiell Hammett Grants

Presented since 1989 to writers around the world
who have been victimized by political persecution.

30 writers from 17 countries
share this year's grants
totalling approximately $175,000

The 1994 recipients include

• Njehu Gatabaki and Pius Nyamora, two Kenyan journalist-publishers harassed, arrested and charged with sedition for covering sensitive political stories.

• Shahrunush Parsipur, an Iranian novelist jailed and prosecuted, and her publisher's offices bombed after publication of her collected stories, *Women Without Men.*

• Nguyen Chi Thiên, a Vietnamese poet, imprisoned for 27 years, now ailing and still under surveillance for portraying people's hardships under the Communist regime.

• Irene Petropoulou, the editor of Greece's oldest gay and lesbian magazine, prosecuted in what she calls a campaign of government harassment, for publishing "incecent and offensive" material.

For a complete listing of the grants and more information, contact Human Rights Watch, 485 Fifth Avenue, New York, NY 10017, USA. Attention: Marcia Allina. Phone (212) 972-8400; Fax (212) 972-0905.

ANNA J ALLOTT

Burmese ways

'Concepts such
as truth, justice
and compassion
are often the only
bulwarks which
stand against
ruthless power.'
Aung San Suu Kyi

(Above) Credit: Charbonnier/Camera Press;
(Left) Credit: Caroline Courtauld

Independence to unfreedom

When Burma regained independence from British rule in January 1948, the economy had barely begun to recover from the devastation of World War II and numerous political groups were vying for power. Under the new parliamentary constitution of 1947, the less extreme left-wing leaders of the Burmese independence movement formed the new government and were immediately faced by various internal rebellions of both Communist and ethnic minority groups, some of which have continued to this day. At this point, the army *(Tatmadaw)* played a vital role in controlling the rebellions, in holding the union together and in helping the new government to survive.

By the end of the 1950s, the governing Anti-Fascist People's Freedom League (AFPFL) had split and, in the general confusion that ensued, the then prime minister, U Nu, was persuaded to hand over power in September 1958 to a 'caretaker' army government headed by General Ne Win. Eighteen months later the army conducted national elections which U Nu's faction won, but by early 1962 the politicians were once again losing popular support and, amid increasing demands for autonomy from some of Burma's ethnic minorities, the army stepped in, ousted the civilian government in a coup on 2 March 1962, and formed a Revolutionary Council to rule the country. This brought to an end the period of parliamentary democracy during which writers and artists had enjoyed almost complete freedom of expression and of the press, and ushered in the period of military rule under which freedom of expression and the right to criticise government policy in public were, step by step, completely suppressed.

In April 1962, the Revolutionary Council put out its policy statement, 'The Burmese Way to Socialism' and, in July, launched its own political party, the Burma Socialist Programme Party (BSPP). The few civilian politicians who agreed to support the Revolutionary Council were mostly of the left, some former Communists; their training in Marxist-Leninist politics and skills with language and propaganda greatly influenced those of the new Burmese brand of socialism.

From February 1963, following a crisis within the Revolutionary Council, the government adopted a less permissive line towards the press: newspaper editors were arrested, the most influential daily paper stopped publication, the government launched its official propaganda paper *Loktha Pyei-thu Nei-zin* (Working People's Daily). Finally, in September 1964, the Revolutionary Council 'resolved the problem of the ownership of the country's main newspapers' by nationalising them but allowing them 'full freedom of expression within the accepted limits of the Burmese Way to Socialism'. One of Asia's freest and most lively presses, with more than 30 daily papers, was extinct.

Henceforth, under the direct control of the Ministry of Information, its task was, and remains, one of 'mass organisation, agitation and objective news dissemination'. Article 157 of the Burmese constitution adopted in 1974 stated: 'Every citizen shall have freedom of speech, expression and publication to the extent that such freedom is not contrary to the interests of the working people and socialism'. For 30 years this has meant that the press — and later radio and television — has been used by the government to explain official policies, inform the people of only those facts it deems important or beneficial and to exhort them to work harder and make do with less.

Until September 1988 the goal was a 'socialist society'; since then the word socialism has disappeared from all official statements — it is sometimes inked out from older texts — and has been replaced by the 'three main causes' — a series of State Law and Order Restoration Council (SLORC) slogans which every book and magazine is obliged to carry on its first or second page. They deface the publications which are forced to print them as much as the large red billboards carrying the same message scar the landscape.

By the beginning of 1988, the Press Scrutiny Board (PSB) had relaxed sufficiently to allow a certain amount of criticism of the government and its management of the economy. Private individuals and organisations were given licences for new monthly magazines — the most lively field of literary activity in Burma. By mid-year, over 90 magazines covering literature, fiction, film, pop music, home and family, religion, foreign news, technical and scientific matters were being published. A licence meant that the Paper and Printing Corporation would release an allocation of paper at the controlled price to the licence holder.

In March, a wave of pro-democracy demonstrations occurred at Rangoon University after the death of a young student, Maung Hpon Maw, at the hands of the riot police. More students were killed, hundreds of others were arrested, and 41 people died in police custody.

On 13 May, the official report of the committee investigating the death of Maung Hpon Maw admitted that the student had indeed been shot by the security forces, that 625 students had been arrested by the end of March, but claimed that by 1 May most of these had been released. The students' protests became stronger and more widely supported through May, June and July. The government was gradually forced by public opinion to give more truthful reports of what had taken place, to admit mistakes and to rescind hastily imposed decrees. By the middle of August, after more bloody confrontations, during which many civilians (some say thousands) died, Maung Maung, a civilian lawyer, took over as president and there was a lull in the violence. On 26 August, Aung San Suu Kyi (the daughter of Aung San, the leader of the post-war independence movement who was assassinated in 1947) addressed her first mass rally at the Shwedagon Pagoda.

On 25, 26 and 27 August, no newspapers appeared. Workers were out demonstrating in support of four demands: the resignation of the government; the formation of an interim government; the holding of multi-party elections; the right to publish freely. The official newspapers which reappeared after the break reported more accurately on recent events. The first unofficial news sheets — around 100 in all — also began to appear, with much fuller detail, graphic, even lurid, photographs, and expressions of personal opinion as people lost their fear and sensed that their demands might be within their grasp. The official press began to carry numerous pictures of peaceful demonstrators marching in Rangoon, lists of their demands and accounts of widespread looting on a massive scale, with shocking incidents of mob revenge. There were also interviews with opposition leaders including Aung San Suu Kyi, feature articles about the BBC's World Service, about the conduct of elections in Western democracies and courageous personal statements by older Burmese journalists, silenced for so long.

But on 16 September, the government ordered all military, police and public servants to resign from the BSPP — many civil servants had already done so — and ordered all striking government employees to return to work. Two days later, amid more bloody confrontations, the army took over the government and General Saw Maung became the chairman of a new ruling body, the State Law and Order Restoration Council (SLORC). Burma has remained under SLORC control ever since, despite the results of the 1990 elections in which the National League for Democracy (NLD), won a commanding victory.

Censorship returned in full strength, accompanied by arrests and imprisonment of writers and intellectuals who had been involved in the democracy movement. In July 1989, Aung San Suu Kyi was put under house arrest and several leading writers who had been actively campaigning with her were arrested. Among the most famous of these were Win Tin (former editor of Mandalay's *Hanthawadi* newspaper), who is still in prison, and Maung Thawka, a poet and writer, who died in prison in June 1991. Some have since been released: Maung Ko Yu (in early 1991), San San Nwe (in mid-1990), Ma Theingi (in April 1992), and Min Lu (in September 1992). By January 1993, as the National Convention began its meetings to prepare for the drafting of the new constitution, it seemed that some of the restrictions were being lifted and more foreign journalists were allowed into Burma. However, in August 1993, two other writers, Aung Khin Sint and Ma Thida, both active members of the NLD, were arrested and sentenced to 20-year prison sentences. PEN Writers in Prison believe 15 writers remain in prison.

After five years...

In most cultures the end of the old year is a time for both spiritual and physical cleansing. It is a time for discarding what is worn out or ill-omened, a time to create an unsullied space for pristine thoughts and new beginnings. Tomorrow is the first of the three days of the Thingyan festival which precedes the Burmese New Year. Thingyan denotes a crossing over from the old to the new.

Education is the bridge that enables us to cross over from redundant mental processes to fresh intellectual vigour. In its best and broadest sense, education is seen not simply as a means of acquiring paper qualifications but as the door to wisdom, the foundation for all that is auspicious. Buddhism associates good deeds with the wise and evil deeds with the foolish and ignorant. Those who seek to remove ignorance help to promote

NLD headquarters: closed down

not only worldly knowledge and spiritual enlightenment but, and this is of the utmost importance, a sense of individual responsibility and self-reliance. Such qualities are urgently needed in contemporary Burma as it passes through a critical period of transition. The choices made at this time will determine the future of the country for years to come. It is therefore essential that our young people should be equipped to rise to the many practical and intellectual challenges which now confront them.

One scholarship is but a drop in the ocean of existing needs. It is my hope that our own people will participate increasingly in the endeavour to gain for our country the benefits of truly meaningful education. It is the most valuable legacy that we can leave to future generations.

Aung San Suu Kyi

First delivered by her husband Dr Michael Aris at a fundraising reception hosted by the educational charity 'Prospect Burma' which will administer the annual scholarship.

ANON

Quite unfair and cruel to boot

I have never heard
That a whole abdomen had to be opened up
Just to cure a mild case of diarrhoea.
I have never heard
That an entire pile of books was burnt
Just because a single termite blighted one.
I have never heard
That a spoilt child was stabbed
Just to scold him for crying for sweets.
I have never heard
That death sentences have been handed down
To minor violators of the Highway Code.
But I have heard that
The odious sentence of a lifetime's transportation
Has been given
For one small offence of rightly being angry
For just one day.

Circulated at the time of the death in prison in 1991
of Maung Thawka, poet and democracy activist

CAROLINE COURTAULD

Inked over, ripped out

When censorship is merely scrutiny and 'restraint' is a virtue devoutly wished, but flouted by the army

The foreign tourists who visit Burma in ever-increasing numbers and who are captivated by its unspoilt beauty and the warm hospitality of its people, can have little idea of the all-embracing and repressive censorship which is suffocating the intellectual life of the country. If the same tourist were to pick one of the numerous monthly magazines on a bookstall and flick through its pages, printed on rough, greyish recycled paper, with no colour except for the cover, the large blocks of blacked out text and patches of silver ink tell their own story. This is the work of the censors or, to give them their official name, the Press Scrutiny Board. The whole pages that have been torn out are not, of course, evident. At times, what has been censored ghosts through the silver paint, revealing what it is the SLORC fears and the strange workings of its collective mind.

In February this year, *Kalyar* magazine carried, in its World Affairs section, a short report about black businessmen in South Africa. Of the two small photographs, one was painted out, as was the name of the victim in the accompanying text. In his speech accepting the Nobel Peace Prize in December 1993, Nelson Mandela — the invisible man — had referred to the captivity of fellow Nobel laureate Aung San Suu Kyi and made a powerful plea for her release.

But the humble clerk carrying out the censor's orders had, perhaps deliberately, not inked over the name 'Mandela', written faintly in English at the foot of the photo. The identity of the banned person was there for all to see, a vivid illustration of the petty vindictiveness and ultimate futility of Burma's censorship.

Last year, the SLORC appeared to believe it could convince the United Nations Commission for Human Rights that the system operated by its Press Scrutiny Board did not amount to censorship. A report by Professor Yozo Yokota, the UN Special Rapporteur for Myanmar on Human Rights, issued in February 1993, stated that he 'was informed that within Myanmar the written press, radio and television continued to be subject to governmental censorship and that the distribution of written material was also subject to governmental limitations and control'. In response the Permanent Representative of Myanmar in Geneva issued a categorical denial. 'It is not true,' he said, 'that there is government censorship of the press, radio and television and distribution of written material. The media, however, are required to restrain themselves from making statements which would disrupt public order and tranquillity. There is the Printers and Publishers Law in Myanmar and it is certainly not unique to Myanmar.'

'The media are required to restrain themselves from making statements which would disrupt public order and tranquillity'

The Printers and Publishers Law referred to by His Excellency was passed by the military government in 1962. Rule 18 states that the name of the printer, his registration number, the name and location of the printing press, the publisher's name, registration number and name and address of the publishing house are to be clearly printed in all publications — books, newspapers, pamphlets, bulletins, periodicals of all kinds. Rule 19 states that the name of the editor must be printed in a prominent place in all newpapers and periodicals.

In 1977, the Printers and Publishers Central Registration Committee of the BSPP issued a new publications directive (no 22) which stated that 'all manuscripts, including novels but excepting periodicals which are published regularly, are to be submitted for prior approval before printing and publication with effect from 9 May 1977.'

All books were to be 'scrutinised' in manuscript before printing; periodicals, including the numerous, widely read fiction and general-interest magazines, were 'scrutinised' after printing just prior to distribution. If a magazine editor wished to avoid the loss of ripped out pages, the cost of having banned portions inked over and the fall in sales owing to failure to appear on time — all of which were to be paid by the editor — it meant remorseless self-censorship.

After the SLORC seizure of power in 1988, but before the 1990 elections and assisted by the spread of photocopiers, a good deal of unscrutinised material of a political nature began to circulate. This prompted the military rulers to issue a new directive (no 38) on 6 June 1989, making it clear that no unscrutinised material of any kind would be allowed to get through. 'At present it is seen that some printers and publishers, some organisations and some persons who are carrying out

---

Are you now or have you ever...

Soon after the award of the Nobel Peace Prize to Aung San Suu Kyi in October 1991, the PSB instituted the 'biographical form'. Its purpose was to flush out banned authors writing under pseudonyms. Together with their manuscripts, authors must submit a completed form stating if they have ever engaged in political activity or served a prison sentence. Failure to submit the form or the answer 'Yes' kills the manuscript. Editors of magazines are required to countersign these forms.

---

printing and publishing work are not abiding by the provisions of Rules 18 and 19 of the law and directive Number 22. Hence, with effect from 6-6-89, the date of the issue of this directive, effective action will be taken, under section 20 of the Printers and Publishers Registration Law of 1962, against printers, publishers, organisations or individuals who, in carrying out printing and publishing work, fail to abide by Rules 18 and 19 and Directive Number 22 issued by the Printers and Publishers Central Registration Committee, dated 7 May 1977.'

Some courageous magazine editors became known for their willingness to print material likely to incur censorship; if they were too daring, however, their magazine was closed down altogether. In December 1991 poet Tin Moe, newly appointed editor of *Pei-hpu-hlwa*, was simultaneously arrested and sentenced to four years in jail.

SUBSCRIPTIONS 1994
United Kingdom & Overseas (excl USA & Canada)

INDEX

ON CENSORSHIP

Lancaster House, 33 Islington High Street
London N1 9LH, UK
tel: 071 278 2313 fax:071-278 1878

1yr	UK:	£30	Overseas: £36	Students: £23 (Worldwide)	
2yr		£55	£66		
3yr		£80	£99		

Yes, I would like to subscribe to **Index on Censorship**.

❏ I enclose a cheque* or money order for **£**..................
(*Sterling cheques must be drawn on a London bank)

❏ Please charge **£**........ to my

    ❏ Visa/Mastercard

    ❏ American Express

    ❏ Diners Club

CARD NUMBER...

....

EXP DT..................

❏ I have instructed my bank to send £..............
to your bank account 0635788 at Lloyds Bank,
10 Hanover Square, London W1R 0BT

SIGNATURE...

NAME...

ADDRESS...

❏ I have sent £.............. to your Post Office
National Giro account 574-5357 (Britain)

....

....

❏ Also, you can send **Index** to a reader in the developing world — for only £18! These sponsored subscriptions promote free speech around the world for only the cost of printing and postage.

SUBSCRIPTIONS 1994
USA & Canada

INDEX

ON CENSORSHIP

Lancaster House, 33 Islington High Street
London N1 9LH, UK
tel: 071 278 2313 fax:071-278 1878

'Index has bylines that Vanity Fair would kill for. Would that bylines were the only things about Index people were willing to kill for.' **BOSTON GLOBE**

1yr	US$	$48	Students: $35
2yr		$90	
3yr		$136	

❏ I enclose a cheque or money order in US$ for **$**................

❏ Please charge **$** ....to my

    ❏ Visa/Mastercard

    ❏ American Express

    ❏ Diners Club

CARD NUMBER...

....

EXP DT..................

SIGNATURE...

NAME...

ADDRESS...

....

....

❏ Also, you can send **Index** to a reader in the developing world — for only $27! These sponsored subscriptions promote free speech around the world for only the cost of printing and postage.

Index on Censorship
Lancaster House
33 Islington High Street
London N1 9LH
United Kingdom

BUSINESS REPLY MAIL

FIRST CLASS   PERMIT NO. 7796   NEW YORK, NY

POSTAGE WILL BE PAID BY ADDRESSEE

INDEX ON CENSORSHIP
c/o HUMAN RIGHTS WATCH
485 FIFTH AVENUE
NEW YORK, NY 10164-0709

The censors are particularly sensitive to any mention of 'democracy' and 'human rights'; neither word is permitted in any text. No attack on or criticism of the Burmese army or of the SLORC is allowed; no writing — even names of characters and story illustrations — which might bring Aung San Suu Kyi and the events of 1988 to mind is permitted; even the mention of former winners of the Nobel Peace Prize is likely to be inked over. The work of writers imprisoned for political reasons may not be reprinted and their names may not appear in print. Since this latter ban can operate restrospectively, if the banned name were to appear in a reprinted work it would be painted out of the text. This retrospective censorship also applies to recent historical writing, where the various Communist groups who were in armed rebellion against the government may no longer be written about as 'rebels' (*thu-bon*) but must be called 'insurgents' (*thaung-gyan-thu*). The word 'rebel' has come to be reserved for one who fights against an oppressive (colonial) regime, while all those who have opposed the Burmese military government since 1962 are simply 'insurgents'.

'Doe-bama': we the Burmese

The censor's interference begins with spelling and includes a prohibition on the use of slang. For example, the spelling of the word *Doe*, 'We, Our' as in *Doe-bama* — 'We, the Burmese' — which evokes a feeling of national pride, may only be used in official publications. Ordinary writers are restricted to using the spelling *toe* which has no nationalist overtones. Similarly, as in the country's renaming, the new, official pronunciation and spellings of various place-names, established by decree in 1989, must be used in all texts: Pagan has become Bagan, Pegu has become Bago, even in Burmese. Burma is Myanmar, the town of Maymyo must be referred to by its original Burmese name, Pyin-oo-lwin. Often the reader is quite unable to imagine what politically dangerous remark can possibly be concealed beneath the silver ink in the middle of a passage of dialogue; it may merely turn out to be the use of the slang expression *yei* to mean 'money' — something like using 'dough' or 'bread' in English.

In a country where television, radio and all newspapers are government-owned and controlled, the vitality of the country's literary and intellectual life can best be judged from the quantity and quality of the monthly magazines, in particular the popular fiction magazines, with their short stories, poems, cartoons and foreign and general news articles. The short stories are the most keenly awaited. Each of 20 or so magazines may carry four to six stories, making the monthly output as much as 100. However, editors are made cautious by the costs of offending the censors.

The PSB works closely with Burmese military intelligence; if it is uncertain about the the current standing of an author — whether he is on the black-list or not — they pass the manuscript on to the military intelligence. The most recent example of censorship is the ripping out in May 1994 of the story 'Human market'*(lu-zei)* — one can only assume it dealt with young Burmese girls sold into prostitution in Thailand, something the government does not admit to.

There are further unpleasant consequences for writers whose story is unexpectedly and without explanation torn out. They are left under a cloud: magazine editors are reluctant to accept their work for fear of themselves incurring banning and financial loss. The arbitrary nature of the banning, the absence of explicit guidelines and the failure to provide reasons, add to the pressures driving authors to censor themselves and editors to ask for changes in their manuscripts, in an attempt to second-guess the PSB. It requires a determined editor to test whether an author remains on some black-list or other by submitting a story for pre-publication censorship. Only if the story comes back passed for publication will the unfortunate author know that he or she is back in the clear. In this area, as in others, fear and uncertainty lead to a reluctance to make decisions or take action.

For a short time in 1990 it looked as if the democracy movement might succeed, and the economy briefly picked up. New magazines started, while suspended ones resumed publication. When the ruling party refused to relinquish power to the victorious democrats, the trend was reversed; foreign investment failed to materialise and the Burmese economy has shown little sign of real growth since — though individual entrepreneurs have become very wealthy. In the face of continuing inflation, the majority of the population finds it hard to make ends meet;

Be more explicit

In 1975, in an effort to reduce the uncertainty about what would and would not pass the PSB, the SLORC issued the following memorandum:

'The Central Registration Board hereby informs all printers and publishers that it has laid down the following principles to be adhered to in scrutinizing political, economic and religious manuscripts, and novels, journals and magazines. They must be scrutinized for the following:

Anything detrimental to the Burmese Socialist Programme; anything detrimental to the ideology of the state; anything detrimental to the socialist economy; anything which might be harmful to national solidarity and unity; anything which might be harmful to security, the rule of law, peace and public order; any incorrect ideas and opinions which do not accord with the times; any descriptions which, though factually correct, are unsuitable because of the time or the circumstances of their writing; any obscene (pornographic) writing; any writing which would encourage crimes and unnatural cruelty and violence; any criticism of a non–constructive type of the work of government departments; any libel or slander of any individual.'

It did nothing to reduce the uncertainty. Throughout the '70s and '80s, Burmese writers continued to face arbitrary decisions aggravated by the '11 prohibitions'.

---

government servants on fixed salaries find it particularly difficult and are obliged to resort to bribes. This type of petty corruption is one of the most frequent targets of the cartoonists.

Book and magazine prices have risen steadily in comparison with salaries, fewer people can afford to buy their own copies and resort to book-hire shops which, bowing to the market, tend to stock only the most popular titles. There is little profit for publishers in more serious titles. Combined with the loss of ideological direction in the wake of the collapse of Communism and the defeat of democracy, the impossibility of recording freely all that they are currently feeling and experiencing in the ever-present climate of censorship, the vitality of Burmese literature has been sapped and its content trivialised.

As is the case with many older writers, the writer Mya Than Tint, for example, once a convinced and active Communist who served several terms in prison in the '50s, '60s and '70s, has become a firm believer in the cause of democracy and human rights. One no longer hears the over-worked slogans 'people's literature', 'writing beneficial for the people', 'taking the side of the masses'. However writers do not yet dare to write openly in support of democracy and human rights. The younger generation has, in any case, no personal experience of freedom of expression or of democracy. The solid ground of 'socialist realism' has become shifting sand and they are forbidden to speak up for an open and democratic system.

Three types of publication have become popular under the present regime: new magazines concerned with business and the free market, religious works and light-weight fiction and love stories. Soon after assuming power in September 1988, the SLORC officially abandoned socialism and announced its new 'open-door' free market economic policy. Three new monthlys dealing with Burmese and world-wide economics, production and manufacture, advertising, management skills, and export opportunities began publication. Most foreign material is translated from English-language publications, but enterprising Burmese journalists have taken full advantage of the opportunity to do some real investigative reporting, previously not allowed, within and on the borders of Burma.

Readers disenchanted by the political situation have turned to religion. They have a choice of about 20 different monthly publications all dealing with Buddhism, some of which officially print 10,000 copies a month, although printings of 70,000 have been unofficially reported.

Fiction mostly concentrates on light-weight love stories, in addition to that dealing with the hardships of everyday life under government mismanagement of the failing economy.

A most censored man

One that got through. Published in 1990, when SLORC were refusing to hand over power. The umbrella is the symbol of royal power.

'Atishoo', 'Coughs'.
'Here you are. Your umbrella.'

'This little book contains my cartoons that were passed for publication between 1981 and 1990. Half my published cartoons were recensored and refused publication when it came to the preparation of this book, hence the few that remain add up to a very small work.'

Inscribed in the front of a copy of his book, sent with a letter to Anna Allott in which he says he thinks he must be 'the most censored cartoonist in Burma'.

Letting the cat out

RICHARD HARRINGTON/CAMERA PRESS

Complicated stories of treacherous machinations and conspiracies by the army

According to the un-written and illogical rules of Burmese censorship, the pages of the government-owned media, and government-financed magazines such as *Myeq-khin-thit,* reveal things the SLORC would much rather its population did not find out. They can write on subjects banned elsewhere — even though these accounts are accompanied by scathing denunciations. In the laborious process of reviling its enemies at home and abroad, the government becomes an important bearer of otherwise banned information.

The SLORC has been forced to start from the assumption that the Burmese people already know a great deal about what is going on in the outside world as well as in Burma thanks to the vernacular services of the British Broadcasting Corporation (BBC), Voice of America (VOA), All India Radio (AIR) and, more recently, satellite TV. Instead of ignoring the broadcasts, the SLORC has felt it necessary to make war on foreign broadcasting by rebuttal, recasting foreign news with an anti-Western and/or pro-Asian slant and denigrating leading members of the opposition party, the National League for Democracy (NLD).

One weapon in the propaganda war was the press conference — later published as books, in both English and Burmese versions — at which the SLORC would attempt to prove that pro-democracy activists were simultaneously in the pay of the CIA and the Burma Communist Party (BCP). The 'evidence' displayed has included photographs of sharpened pencils, wigs and women's clothing seized from dissident monasteries.

The books-of-the-conferences, with catchy titles like *The Conspiracy of Treasonous Minions within the Myanmar Naing-ngan* and *Traitorous Cohorts Abroad and Web of Conspiracy: Complicated Stories of Treacherous Machinations and Intrigues of BCP UG, DAB and some NLD Leaders to Seize State Power* provided some Burmese with the only news and pictures they could get about relatives who were involved in Burmese expatriate groups. [BCP UG refers to underground members of the Communist party of Burma the DAB is the Democratic Alliance of Burma, an umbrella grouping of mostly ethnic minority opposition movements.]

Another series of books which must soon become collector's items was *A Skyful of Lies*. BBC, VOA and AIR broadcasts were reprinted, first in the newspapers and then in collected form, for the SLORC to rebut — and in the process enable Burmese to catch up on the previous night's BBC broadcast in the pages of the official press. The population has long since ceased to believe in its newspapers, as Min Lu observed in his poem 'What Has Become of Us?':

Having tricked the people into closing their eyes, those in power deprive them of what should rightfully be theirs

Although they have abolished the one-party system in Burma
We still live in a single paper dictatorship
Where the *Working People's Daily*
Leaves a bitter taste in our mouths.

Some people say that
There is not a single true news item
In the *Working People's Daily*.
But it's not really that bad.
There is some news which is 50 per cent true
(I'm only talking about the weather forecast of course)
And once a month there is 100 per cent reliable information
(When they announce the lottery winners).

Times have changed since Min Lu wrote in 1990. The Burmese New Year in 1993 saw the tabloid *Working People's Daily* renamed *The New Light of Myanmar*, now a broadsheet and computer typeset. There are now several other daily newspapers, *The Mirror* and *City News* in Rangoon and *Yadanabon Daily* in Mandalay. Continuous propaganda has given way to more sport, more culture and articles on business reprinted from the previous day's *Straits Times* of Singapore.

Myeq-khin-thit (New Pastures), a propaganda magazine founded in 1990, numbers among its stock-in-trade regular nationalist and anti-

'*The preceding news was not true.*' '*Hmm! Then it must be true.*'

colonialist articles; an 'Any Questions?' section designed to insult pro-democracy activists; fiction, usually with a pro-government angle; regular features reviling the West and its human rights hypocrisy; and much in support of government activities. Poems and cartoons, are often culled from other magazines and reprinted without permission.

Although some Burmese intellectuals consider *Myeq-khin-thit* beneath

---

Some thoughts on satellite

'Now that the Ministry of Communications has announced that it is necessary for satellite users to inform the township and register, as it were, in order to be able to use a satellite dish lawfully, the number of people fixing them up and using them openly and boldly has increased. There is a tremendous run on satellite dishes. The cost of installation all in (everything fixed up and working well) will be about 80,000 to 100,000 *kyat* — well beyond the means of most people.

Some people install their dishes so that they can't be seen; others place them prominently on their roof top, pointing to the east in the direction of the satellite. Some people are very pleased to be able to watch transmissions around the clock for 24 hours — they tune into Hong Kong and Bangkok programmes. Others, having heard the rumours that the cost will be about 2,400 *kyat* per month, are unwilling to pay so much.

However, since the electricity supply in Mandalay is restricted, the people who live in the run-of-the-mill areas of the town cannot even venture to think about installing dishes. The main preoccupations of the mass of the population in Mandalay are that the price of rice should come down and the electricity supply be constant and regular.'

From an independent Rangoon monthly

---

contempt, it does have the advantage of never being subjected to scrutiny. It can use stronger language than other magazines, and can be more controversial. Its style and techniques are those of the Western tabloid press and as long as the government censors other monthly magazines, people will wade through the propaganda and smears to get to the news they are banned from reading elsewhere.

WIN PE

Barapi

EVER since Ba Chay was little, he'd never had any family. He had been brought up in a monastery in the village of Lime-pond. Once he was grown up, he took to hauling water for a living. Hauling water for a living in Lime-pond was the worst job there was. Almost the entire population used to go down to the stream at the edge of the village to wash their clothes and bathe and the village had, in any case, several wells, so it was rare to find someone who would pay to have water carried for them.

Why, then, did Ba Chay haul water for a living in this particular village? It was simple. Ba Chay was not very bright, he had never learned anything at school and he couldn't think things out for himself. It was the only job he could do.

He very rarely received any money. Mostly when he did a job, he would be paid in whatever he needed at the time. This was because people usually employed him because they felt sorry for him. If he had been prepared to fetch and carry, dig and hoe, he could have got more money than he did from hauling water, but — and I don't know whether you should just call him unlucky or whether he was just a dimwit — he had been bequeathed a yoke and water buckets by Grandpa Aba-shin, the old water carrier, and he took up water carrying as if it were his natural task in life. He seemed to believe that no other work had anything to do with him. He was simple and he was gormless; this job was his life and that was all there was to it.

However, he would always do whatever jobs the senior monk of the monastery asked him to. After all, that wasn't work, that was looking after his own teacher. The senior monk used to give him the left-overs from the monastery. Ba Chay would get all sorts of things to eat, though for none of them did he feel a particular fondness.

One day, the monk passed on to Ba Chay a sort of Indian snack

which he had been offered by an almsgiver from Mandalay. It is known as
'*barapi*' in Upper Burma, and is made with cream from the top of the
milk. As soon as the food touched his tongue, Ba Chay got goosebumps
all over. Never before had he tasted such a divine combination of
sweetness and cream. He knew immediately that this had to be manna
from heaven, the same as the *nats* ate! He decided at once that this was
what it must be.

After only one small mouthful, Ba Chay became hooked on this
creamy *barapi*. Since the monk had left him barely a square inch of the
stuff, he was dying to eat more. You know how it is: when you can't get
enough of something it becomes all the more desirable. After eating the
barapi, he downed a glass of cold water and the taste in his mouth became
even more sensational.

That day, when he told the villagers in his artless manner that he had
eaten manna from heaven, left for him by the monk, they were very
amused. And from that day on, when the village monk or anyone else
with money happened to be passing through Mandalay and managed to
pick up some *barapi*, they would remember Ba Chay and save some for
him. No matter how many times he ate the stuff, he never tired of it. It
became even more addictive. In spite of everyone telling him over and
over again that it was called *barapi* or *malain-ge*, poor old Ba Chay still
called it 'manna', 'manna from heaven' through force of habit. If
someone was going to Mandalay and Ba Chay had managed to save up a
bit of money, he would ask them to buy him some manna — I mean
barapi. If they brought some back with them, he would be delighted.
After he had eaten the manna and washed it down with water, the world
seemed a beautiful and pleasant place, quite blissful and devoid of pain.

However, Ba Chay's increasing addiction to the stuff had started to
take hold of him like a disease. He began to worry frantically that he
might die without one last taste of *barapi*. He became obsessed with the
idea that death would only be worthwhile if he could die while relishing
the delectable taste of *barapi* in his mouth.

One day dacoits raided Lime-pond. They fired non-stop at anything
that moved and the inhabitants of the village fled for their lives and hid.
At that moment, Ba Chay thought he would surely die. But there was a
problem: he didn't have any *barapi*. When he realised that he was about to

die and that *barapi* would not be the last thing he ate before dying, he became very agitated. However, the dacoits left the village and Ba Chay was out of danger. Thank goodness for that!

From then on, every time he bought some *barapi,* he would put a little aside for a rainy day, so that if he was taken ill with a fever, he would be able to eat some before he died. This proved to be no small problem. When he did get a fever, in addition to all the chest congestion, eating this creamy sweet made him even sicker. Luckily he wasn't in a position to eat lots of it.

When the time came around for him to dredge out the well in the monastery compound, one of the monks warned him that if one was unlucky, one could die going down the well, either of a stroke or suffocation. If that was the case, said Ba Chay, he wasn't going down until he'd had some *barapi*. He wouldn't calm down until the abbot had scolded him for being so silly, and even then, descended the well full of fear. He wasn't afraid of dying — oh no. He was afraid of dying without a taste of *barapi*.

AFTER Ba Chay had turned 30, his luck changed. If you'll excuse my bluntness — Ma Sein Yin, the unmarried owner of the only cheroot factory in town, took a fancy to him. She took to calling him round for a variety of supposed reasons. But Ba Chay was such a simpleton he would only go to her house if she was hiring him to carry water for her. As a result, Ma Sein Yin would hire him every day to bring in her bath water. This was all a bit ludicrous because Ma Sein Yin, who had at one time gone down to the stream to wash, along with the rest of the village, had built a bathroom in her compound near the well, which she said she would be using for washing in. This kind of thing was very unusual in Lime-pond. In any case, she had a cheroot factory full of employees. Yet she insisted on getting Ba Chay to bring her water. The whole village rapidly caught on to Ma Sein Yin's real intentions, but she herself was not embarrassed at all and paid no attention to what her neighbours thought.

Waiting to wash, with her *longyi* tucked up round her breasts and a towel draped over her bare shoulders, she would watch Ba Chay from close quarters as he scooped the water for her, admiring his muscles as they glistened with sweat. For about two months she bathed like this.

After that, Ba Chay moved in with Ma Sein Yin. Criticism and praise are short-lived creatures, however, and after a month, the wagging tongues were still.

From that time, since he was now the husband of Ma Sein Yin, the cheroot factory owner, Ba Chay no longer needed to haul water. I won't bother mentioning that the attraction of *barapi* was one of the many ruses she employed. Ba Chay had now reached the point where he could eat *barapi* every day. Ma Sein Yin had found herself a love-potion to keep her man satisfied for life.

THERE was only one matter that might have presented a slight problem for Ma Sein Yin, namely that from time to time, a group of rich men from Mandalay with a taste for hunting used to come and camp out in her house. But being men of the world, this group from the city thought

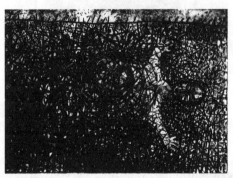

VLADIMIR SIELADCOU

nothing of Ba Chay's presence in the house. They treated him as they would anyone else, and didn't look down on him. They simply saw him as the husband of the house-owner. This was a weight off Ma Sein Yin's mind. Only Ko Tin Tun, a sugar-refiner who had on and off been discreetly wooing Ma Sein Yin, was a little put out.

But most important of all, this group had caught word of Ba Chay's reputation and consequently every time they were about to set off for the country, they stocked up on *barapi* for him. So there was not the slightest problem and since Ba Chay was happy, so was Ma Sein Yin.

As time passed, Ba Chay and the hunting group became close friends and, one day when they were preparing to go hunting in the jungle between Water Sycamore Lake and the Kayla range, he decided to go with them. However, entering the jungle is a dangerous thing and one might well meet one's end. It was most important, therefore, that Ba Chay should stock up on *barapi,* and he calculated before leaving that he would need enough for two nights and three days.

They set off on the fourth waning day of the full moon of *Tabaung* and reached the camp safely that evening. However, as Ko Tin Tun had told them they should avoid referring to it as the 'waning' moon, but should use the words 'past the full moon', they were all a little jittery. Ba

VLADIMIR SIELADCOU

Chay, with the least schooling, was more nervous than the rest.

Nonetheless, that night they enjoyed themselves eating and drinking. As the night grew later and they were about to turn in, their world was suddenly turned upside down. A herd of wild elephants charged their camp and they had to flee pell-mell. The inky darkness of the night added to their problems. They were forced to run headlong, blindly tripping and stumbling. Scratched and stabbed by thorns and branches, covered in wounds, they could hear each other's screams and shouts from here and there in the darkness. It was impossible to find anywhere to take cover; each time the great black shapes loomed out of darkness, accompanied by the sound of snapping branches, they had to flee for their lives. There was no time to think about where they were or where they were going — they just had to take to their heels and run.

Two or three hours later, all had fallen silent. Ba Chay found himself lying exhausted in a bush where he had taken cover as best he could. It was so dark he couldn't even see his hand in front of his face. His whole body ached all over, and blood oozed from his many wounds. But he couldn't be concerned about that, he just lay still and tried to get his breath back. Drifting in and out of consciousness, he finally fell asleep.

Who can say what time he woke up. Maybe the scorching heat of the sun woke him, or perhaps he simply regained consciousness. Opening his eyes with great effort, he saw first the customary blur which gradually cleared to reveal leafless branches against a blinding white sky. Other than that he could see nothing. He tried to turn his head to look around him, but couldn't move. He tried again, but without success. He tried to move his arms and legs but could only manage a slight movement in his left hand. He tried to yell with all his might, but nothing happened when he opened his mouth. Then he heard a noise.

Shortly afterwards, the head of an elephant reared suddenly into view. Ba Chay couldn't move, he couldn't scream, the only movement came from the ever-widening whites of his eyes. Suddenly, his line of sight was blocked by the elephant's foot. Ba Chay felt a dull blow and his body lurched to one side, squashing his face into the branches of the bush. He still couldn't move his head, but his position had shifted and he now had an uninterrupted view towards the foot of the mountain, which also contained the back of the departing elephant. He was certain that he had been trampled by the elephant but he felt no particular pain.

Although he couldn't move, he had retained the use of some of his senses. The elephant had put a foot through his stomach and now he could feel his whole body crawling with ants, swarming and teeming all over him. He was certainly about to die.

Certain to die!? His *barapi!* Where was the *barapi?*

He had none! and there was no way of getting any! There was nothing he could do. Ba Chay was about to die without having eaten a last bite of *barapi.* He had lived out this horrifying situation before. But this time, it was different. Even though he was going to die without eating a last piece of *barapi,* he found that it didn't matter. It made no difference. About two minutes later, Ba Chay breathed his last.

Biographical note:

Win Pe is one of Burma's most popular story-tellers. Now in his mid-50s, he is, on his own admission, something of a jack-of-all-trades: he has at times been a journalist, cartoonist, gem dealer, musician, arts administrator, film director, painter and writer. He grew up in an artistic family and learned Burmese classical music before he began primary school. He studied at Mandalay University, but he left without a degree because, as he said in an interview, he was 'painting, making music and involved in politics.' His first job was as a cartoonist on a left-wing daily newspaper; when the paper was nationalised he went to work in the jade mines owned by his father-in-law. At the age of 31 he was appointed to the post of principal of the State School for Fine Arts, Music and Dancing in Mandalay under the Ministry of Culture, under the Burmese Way to Socialism. Six years later he began to make films.

Win Pe's short stories, which he started to write in the 1980s, are written during breaks in his filming schedules. Many are amusing sketches of mostly male Burmese life, told in simple language, rich in dialogue and comic situations. They are often set in the teashops which are the venue for what remains of political debate in Burma. Since 1991, teashop owners have been told that they will be held personally responsible for anyone found discussing anti-government politics on their premises, and the omni-present informers have practically stifled discussions. Though he now lives in Rangoon with his wife and five children, he still writes mainly about Mandalay and the surrounding towns and villages of Upper Burma.

The story translated here, as with many others, may seem on first reading to be an account of a fairly unimportant event happening to ordinary folk. But situations change rapidly and what was simple becomes complicated, violent, brutal, tragic, above all unexpected. It is often possible to discern a political message within the text; events in the story become a metaphor for the behaviour of the government and army or for the state to which they have reduced the nation, striking familiar chords with readers.

'Barapi' is from his second collection of stories, published in November 1992. The characteristic humour has become more sardonic; the theme of violence and violent death more frequent. As a Burmese critic commented, from his deceptively simple, often comic, narratives emerge powerful images of the greed, anger and stupidity of human life.

MARTIN SMITH

Unending war

For 50 years, Burma's ethnic groups have fought army and government for recognition of their language, culture and ancient learning

It is many years since Burma's once flourishing media reflected the country's vibrant ethnic mosaic. This is due in large part to the countrywide insurrections which broke out after independence in 1948 — as many as 20 ethnic opposition forces, including the Karen National Union (KNU), remain under arms today — but has been exacerbated by a quarter of a century of one-party rule under General Ne Win, who seized power in a military coup in 1962 and sought to impose a highly-Burmanised identity on the country under his monolithic *Burmese Way to Socialism*.

Over 100 different ethnic sub-groups and dialects have been identified amongst Burma's 43 million population, one-third of them ethnic minorities. Many are the descendants of unique cultures which have survived into the 20th century. These include the Nung-Rawang crossbow hunters in the snow-capped mountains of Burma's far north, the Salum sea-gypsies of sub-tropical Tenasserim, and the 'long-necked' Kayans (Padaungs) of the Shan/Karenni borderlands. There are also large minority communities, numbering over 1.5 million, speaking a variety of Chinese and Indian dialects. But, in general, most indigenous languages or dialects in Burma can be broadly categorised into four major linguistic families — the Tibeto-Burman, Mon-Khmer, Shan (Tai) and Karen.

In literary terms, a further distinction can also be made between the main Buddhist groups, notably Mon and Burman, who evolved their own scripts from Sanskritic models in the monasteries many centuries ago, and formerly non–literate hill peoples, such as the Chin and Kachin, who only devised their own writing systems after the British annexation of Burma in the 19th century.

Legends abound among the hill peoples to account for the historical absence of written literatures. A typical but popular story is the Karen legend of the 'Golden Book of Knowledge', stolen by their 'white man' younger brother who returned many years later with the Bible.

Home of ethnic strife

Certainly the arrival of Christian missionaries at the same time as the British led to an explosion in national awareness among many minorities and a dangerous sense of ethnic polarisation from the Burman majority who never really accepted the confines of British rule.

Within a few years, new scripts following a variety of Burmese (eg Karen) or Romanised (eg Kachin) models had been devised, and were swiftly followed by the first periodicals and magazines. As early as 1841, a Karen newspaper, *Sah Tu Ghaw* (Morning Star), was established in Tavoy which, until shut down by Ne Win in 1962, was Burma's longest-running vernacular newspaper. In 1873 the first Rakhine newspaper was produced in Arakan. Another popular paper was *Hongsawadoi,* published in Mon, the country's oldest surviving written language newspaper.

Despite the insurrections, Burma's minority presses continued to expand in the short–lived parliamentary era of 1948-62 when there were over 30 daily newspapers, including six in Chinese and several in Indian languages. In government areas, the publication of popular Mon or Karen language papers, such as *Danangsoi (Tenasserim)* and *Taw-meh-pah*, was halted due to the fighting. But though government censorship was increasing, ethnic minority languages continued to be well represented by a host of different periodicals and magazines. Such publications generally reflected cultural interests: Pao and Mon magazines, for example, were often concerned with Buddhism.

Language was also one of the main focal points of burgeoning nationalist movements among ethnic minorities who, until then, had largely escaped the worst of the fighting. Perhaps the most dramatic cultural renaissance took place in the Shan State in the mid-1950s when students and scholars formed new literary societies to publish Shan-language books and magazines, such as the *Khitthit Shan Pye* journal. Under the patronage of Sao Shwe Thaike, the first president of Burma, the Shan script and traditional Shan theatre were revived and, by the early 1960s, most towns boasted theatre troupes which re-enacted popular folk-tales and classical legends.

During the same period, a similar nationalist revival took place in the Kachin State where the Kachin Youth Culture Uplift Association was formed by a local school headmaster, Brang Seng, who today heads the Kachin Independence Organisation (KIO), one of Burma's most powerful armed opposition groups.

This heady period of cultural experimentation and expression came to an abrupt end with General Ne Win's seizure of power in 1962. Though the Burma Socialist Programme Party's 1974 constitution guaranteed the right of every citizen to 'freely use one's language and literature', ethnic minority languages were one of the main victims of press nationalisation and the security clampdown.

In addition to scrutiny, publications in minority languages also had to pass the additional hurdle of translation into Burmese, a time-consuming and costly operation which discouraged many writers even further.

Censors even complained over translations of the Bible which, they claimed, incited ethnic minorities like the Karens and Kachins to political violence. As a result, minority-language newspapers disappeared altogether, and the remaining publications were reduced to little more than folksy or domestic magazines like the Karen-language *Leh Su Nyah* (Go Forward).

An equal grievance to many ethnic minorities was the treatment of their languages in the education system. Few ethnic nationalists disputed the centrality or importance of Burmese as the common language of Burma. But even today, minority languages are still not used (and then only rarely) beyond fourth grade in primary school.

Not only is such discrimination a major disadvantage to minority children who have to learn to compete in Burmese from their first day in school, but for over three decades it has greatly inhibited the natural development and expression of minority cultures. Historical and religious studies have been equally repressed: university departments such as anthropology have collapsed, and with the exception of the Institute of Foreign Languages in Rangoon, where Chinese is taught, there is no official study of any minority language.

Nonetheless, despite these obstacles, minority languages continue to survive. Around the country there is no shortage of student volunteers for the few community or ethnic group magazines (largely cultural associations) which do receive occasional permission to print.

Meanwhile in territory controlled by the country's diverse armed ethnic nationalist forces, for much of the past four decades underground presses have regularly published in a variety of different languages, including Pao, Kayah and Shan. The quality is generally low, most magazines consisting of little more than political propaganda and news-related commentaries. Among the most consistent publications in recent years have been the *Baknoi Bat Shiga* of the KIO, *Than Noo Htoo* of the KNU and *Rhemmonya* of the New Mon State Party (NMSP).

The growing numbers of peace talks in recent months between many of these groups and the ruling SLORC in Rangoon, leave the future of minority languages and publishing as uncertain as ever. Since April 1992, however, when General Than Shwe replaced General Saw Maung as the SLORC chairman, there have been gradual signs of changes on ethnic minority policy.

Ceasefires have now been agreed with over 10 armed ethnic opposition groups, including the KIO, which for over 30 years had been denounced by successive governments as 'terrorists', 'bandits' or 'drug-smugglers' to be 'annihilated'.

Ethnic minority parties are still cautious, especially while the political situation appears deadlocked in the country at large. There are also important armed forces, such as the KNU, who are yet to agree to peace talks. But it is clear from details of these first discussions that a younger generation of leaders in Burma are aware that the issues of language and cultural expression will be one of the main litmus-tests for ethnic minority citizens if a real peace is ever to come after so many years of bloodshed. 'After all, the Burmese army is also multi-ethnic,' one SLORC official privately said.

Tangible evidence of these changes is still slight, but in the last three years Myitkyina College in the Kachin State and Lashio College in the Shan State have been upgraded to 'degree-colleges', equivalent to university status. More significantly, last year the SLORC released Nai Keythara, a Buddhist monk and poet, who had reportedly received a seven-year prison sentence for illegally trying to promote publishing

SARAH WEBB BARRELL/CAMERA PRESS

United rebel army: a life at war

in the Mon language. In apparent settlement of another long-standing grievance, Mon monks have also recently reported that from this year they will once again be allowed to sit their exams in Mon, the historic language by which Buddhism was brought to Burma.

'They may be small steps,' said Nai Tin Aung, foreign affairs spokesman of the NMSP, 'but at least they are steps in the right direction.'

Whatever the immediate future, the polarised nature of ethnic conflict in Burma over the past five decades has left the aspiring writer a difficult legacy. Many have, nevertheless, tried to address these issues and, particularly among the younger generation, popular culture cuts across ethnic lines.

One of the most popular song-writers in Burma today is the ethnic

Shan, Sai Hti Hseng, who formed a band, the 'Wild Ones' (*Thabawa Yinthwenge*), with fellow Mandalay University students back in 1973. For over 20 years their inspiring lyrics, with a discreet social message, have reached across the generations on all sides of the ethnic divide, showing that a multi-cultural life in Burma can be possible. One of their most poignant but memorable songs takes its name from the band:

If you believe in tomorrow more than today
Then you can come to where hope is the thing
If you're the one who seeks to live a better way
Then you can hear the Wild Ones sing.

Films, video and the reading public

Television came relatively late to Burma in 1980; however there has long been a flourishing indigenous film industry since the 1920s. Since 1988 the shortage of foreign exchange and the cost of film stock has led to a huge increase in the production of video-films. Many writers, including some who are or have been banned, find an alternative source of income in writing scripts for video-films. These must be passed by the Film Scrutiny Board, but a script by a banned author will not necessarily be refused because the author is forbidden to publish his writing.

During the 90s, video-films have become immensely popular throughout the country, even in the remotest villages. Twenty-one, 24 and 28-inch TV sets are installed in a large room or in a specially constructed covered enclosure in the village where 50-60 people at a time can watch for a few pence. If the village has no electricity, the set is run on a privately owned generator. Uncensored foreign videos, brought in through Thailand and China, are in great demand, as are banned copies of Aung San Suu Kyi's 1990 electioneering journeys.

From time to time government officials crack down on unauthorised videos and confiscate large numbers. Since the few public reading rooms tend to stock only government publications, mostly read their comic-books, novels and magazines by borrowing them from small private lending libraries for a tiny daily fee. Today, these are paralled in almost every town and village by video shops, and readership is falling to the competition. Most of the country's favourite film stars and directors are now making video films, but the cost of hiring a made-in-Burma video is two to three times that of a foreign one.

Mandalay 1994

Announcement from retired President Ne Win

4 May 1992

To whom it may concern — an appeal from retired President Ne Win:
You are kindly requested to remove any pictures of me which are hanging in military, departmental or government offices and also not to hang any of the aforesaid pictures on your walls in future.
Signed: Ne Win
Translation from the back pages of the *Working People's Daily* 5-5-92

TIN MOE   *'Fighting peacocks — come to*
our rescue!
Sharpen your claws
File down your spurs
Fight for our path to freedom.'
Tin Moe

The years we didn't see the dawn

Half asleep, half-awake, a time of
dreaming dreams
I wanted to walk but did not know which road to take.
Half unknowing, my days are running out
My paunch thickens and my neck folds sag as I grow older,
A time of getting nowhere. I have passed through all this time
Unheeding, as in a train one passes stations by.

As a young man, I met with Lenin
But growing older, I would like to meet Lincoln....

The way we live now, submitting reports loaded with lies,
Recording 'yes, sir, certainly, sir' onto tapes filled with
misinformation,
Our smart ' party' jackets now all creased and musty.
We are treated like tea-flasks, put here, sent there at our bosses'
bidding,
Robots, our lives without joy, we merely nod our heads.
At this time, we are not poetry, we are not human,
This is not life, this is just so much wastepaper...

We have bartered away our lives for falsehood
And now we have reached old age, at death's very door,
Surely these times should be put on record as
'The years we didn't see the dawn'?

Biographical note:

Tin Moe *(real name U Ba Gyan) was born in 1933. He has published books of poetry, children's poems, and educational books. After 1988 he became a member of the National League for Democracy (NLD) and published a number of poems about the democracy movement. In late 1991 he was appointed editor-in-chief of the flagging* Pe-Hpu-Hlwa *literary magazine, but was arrested in December 1991 after only one issue and the magazine was closed. After being held without charge for six months, he is thought to have been sentenced to four years in June 1992 for allegedly contravening the 1962 Printers and Publishing Law.*

'The years we didn't see the dawn' was written shortly after the military assumption of power in September 1988 and appears to have been first recited by the author at a memorable meeting held by the NLD on 9 December 1988 — the last of the traditional annual lectures, or mass literary rallies that celebrated Writers' Day. These were the only occasions on which writers could communicate directly with their reading public without being subject to censorship. After September 1988 they were stopped — except for the NLD meeting for members only. The chair was taken by Win Tin and the keynote lecture on poetry as a source of inspiration to the nation was given by Tin Moe. Maung Thawka also spoke. Win Tin and Tin Moe are still in prison; Maung Thawka died in prison in 1991.

Bibliography:

Inked Over, Ripped Out; Burmese Storytellers and the Censors by Anna J Allott (PEN American Center, September 1993)

Myanmar (Amnesty International, October 1993)

Myanmar:Human rights developments July to December 1993 (Amnesty International, January 1994)

State of Fear: Censorship in Burma (Article 19, 1991)

Burma Culture Shock! A Guide to Customs and Etiquette by Saw Myat Yin (Kuperard, 1994)

'Well, yes. Your nib may indeed be good and sharp, but ...'

BOOK REVIEWS

DAVID MILLER

The media: a user's manual

Manufacturing Consent: Noam Chomsky and the Media Edited by Mark Achbar, Montréal, Québec, Black Rose Books, 1994, 265pp. £11.99
Censored: The News That Didn't Make the News and Why: The 1994 Project Censored Yearbook. Carl Jensen and Project Censored, New York, Four Walls Eight Windows, 1994, 318pp. US$14.95/£10.99

Everyone is opposed to censorship, yet there is a curious lack of agreement about exactly what defines the censorious act. The clearest cases are direct state interference with the concomitant employment of large numbers of official censors. In liberal democracies direct censorship is most evident in times of war, as we saw in the 1991 Gulf conflict. But the charge of censorship is often rejected in even the clearest examples. Many governments deny that their information controls amount to censorship: the British government denies that the ban on broadcasting statements by Sinn Fein and other Irish organisations amounts to censorship; the Allied forces in the Gulf insisted that information was controlled for reasons of operational security.

Attempts to legitimate the use of censorship are not always successful, nor, as far as the public is concerned, are they always necessary. The British government has recently managed to get the ban on Sinn Fein past the European Commission on Human Rights. Tactically this involved the use of direct censorship inscribed in the law, together with the double-think claim that the ban was not censorship since it placed responsibility for its implementation on the broadcasters. Nervous broadcasters themselves extended the ban and the government could then claim this was nothing to do with them.

Censorship is a contested category. One person's censorship is another person's national security or religious custom. Project Censored operate with a significantly wider definition than direct state censorship. Their book, subtitled *The News That Didn't Make the News*, is a catalogue of media failures together with a resource guide and chronology of censorship. Here censorship refers to news which does not receive prominence in the mainstream media. Among the 25 top censored stories of 1993 are some important suppressed stories. One example is the US intervention in Somalia, which was efficiently portrayed by the US and the BBC as a 'humanitarian' operation. There was little coverage in the US that discussed the potentially huge oil reserves in Somalia which had already been allocated to four big US oil companies before the pro-US president, Siad Barre, was overthrown. The increasingly key role of the public relations industry in skewing news coverage is singled out, as is the role of the CIA in masterminding drug running with elements of the Haitian police.

THIS MODERN WORLD by TOM TOMORROW

What remains to be explained is why and how some stories that, by normal journalistic criteria would merit extensive treatment, come to languish on the inside pages of the press and in alternative publications. This is where *Manufacturing Consent: Noam Chomsky and the Media*, comes in. Subtitled 'A primer in intellectual defense', it is the companion book to the award-winning film of the same name and contains a complete transcript of the film together with excerpts from Chomsky's writings and interviews with him, his critics and others such as co-author Edward Herman.

Chomsky and Herman advance a propaganda model in which there are five major filters through which news must pass 'leaving only the cleansed residue fit to print'. This is expounded at greater length in their *Manufacturing Consent: The Political Economy*, written in 1988 and in Chomsky's *Necessary Illusions: Thought Control in Democratic Societies* a year later.

The filters are the size, concentrated ownership, owner wealth and profit orientation of the dominant mass-media firms; advertising as the primary income source of the mass media; media reliance on official sources; 'flak' as a means of disciplining the media; and 'anticommunism' as a national religion and control mechanism. All these result in major constraints on media practice in Western countries. In Britain, as I have already mentioned, there is also direct state censorship, together with a growing deployment of the law against journalists. These filters enable governments or business elites to manage events in their own interests. While Chomsky and Herman offer a persuasive account of the filters which operate to close down the media, they tend to neglect the factors which can result in the powerful being discomfitted by the media.

Both books focus attention on business and state elites and on the media as the prime agents of censorship by omission or commission. Yet in an introduction to Project Censored's book, celebrated investigative journalist Jessica Mitford devotes most space not to big business or government but to an attack on feminist campaigners against the pornography industry. Much of her invective is a personal attack on Andrea Dworkin and Catherine MacKinnon — hardly comparable in their efforts with the might of the US state. Mitford's introduction alerted me to what seems to be a key ambiguity in these and many otherdiscussions of censorship: should freedom of expression be an absolute right?

Libertarians like Chomsky argue for virtually no censorship. There are, he says, two positions on freedom of speech: freedom for views you like and freedom for those you don't. He has defended the right to freedom of speech for revisionist historians of the Holocaust as well as for war criminals — Nazi leaders and post-war US presidents. Although Chomsky does set limits — the difficulty of continuing to justify academic freedom for counterinsurgency research that results in mass slaughter in the developing world, for example — he has a wider notion of free speech than most of his critics, including some free speech organisations. He has no time for civil liberties and free expression organisations that want to prohibit 'hate speech' or curb glorifications of sexual violence. And yet, the problem of ensuring that freedom of speech or action does not interfere with the exercise of freedom by others remains. Mary Wolstonecraft, who is quoted here, had it about right when she defined freedom, 200 years ago, as 'a degree of liberty, civil and religious, as is compatible with the liberty of every other individual with whom he is united in a social compact, and the continued existence of the compact.'

The two books together make a valuable contribution to 'intellectual self-defence'. Jensen's is, perhaps understandably, predominantly focused on the US; *Manufacturing Consent*, with its wealth of well presented argument, information and critique, gives a more rounded account of the processes by which news and information come to be shaped and makes a valuable teaching aid to accompany the film of the same name.

However, intellectual self-defence does not depend solely on books like these. As Chomsky puts it, 'It's not a matter of what you read, it's a matter of how you read... People have to understand that there's a major effort being made to manipulate them. That doesn't mean the facts aren't there.'

IRENA MARYNIAK

Outsiders in Russia

Glas issue 6: Jews and Strangers, edited by Natasha Perova, Glas Publishers, 1994, Moscow 119517, PO Box 47, Russia *or* c/o Dept of Russian Literature, University of Birmingham, B15 2TT, UK

In Russian the word *sobornost'* conveys the perfectly integrated community, unanimously bound by cultural and religious values, through which personal wilfulness is reoriented towards the Greater Good. It was an ideal espoused, particularly, by the Slavophiles: the purist patriots of 19th century Russia. They held that the country had a unique historical destiny and moral status in the world.

Today, the Slavophile vision, tinged with messianic hopes, still retains an attraction for many Russians as they look for cohesion and identity in a fragile and fragmented political environment. And it is tainted, as ever, with a tendency to categorise everyone by nationality: French means frivolous and superficial; German — schematic and unimaginative; Polish — infantile and vain; Jewish — cunning and mercenary. Clichés which have lost their piquancy in the West remain, in much of Eastern Europe, the benchmarks by which people make sense of the world.

The literary journal *Glas,* one of the few carriers of new Russian writing in translation, recently devoted its sixth issue to the theme of outsiders, exclusion and inner exile. It is entitled 'Jews and Strangers'. Unusually for *Glas,* it spans over a century of prose and poetry, from the 1880s to the present, proving how little some things have changed. And it attempts to address one of the chief preoccupations of fallen empires: who are 'we'? Where do 'we' end and 'others' begin: psychologically, geographically, politically? This is another of those dilemmas which fill the pages of Tolstoy and Dostoevsky and continue to be the subject of impassioned arguments in contemporary politics. For it is precisely in Russia, the land 'beyond all rules and limits' where words, feelings and promises are fluid as the rouble that, as Lev Anninsky writes in *Glas,* 'the most desperate attempts are made to retain one's identity, to withstand this overpowering fusion of colours... The call of the ancestral homeland is one of the last life-saving footholds.'

In 1988, after decades of being refused the right to emigrate, Russian Jews began to leave for Israel in droves. The desire to go was heightened by the loss of the protection the Soviet state had offered, mitigating the sporadic cultural, educational and professional restrictions it had also imposed. In the Soviet Union, a Jewish background was a shaming liability best ignored or forgotten, as Liudmilla Ulitskaya's nicely shaped and keenly observed story '1953' illustrates. The humiliation of expo-

DMITRY PEISAKHOV/CAMERA PRESS

Kiev 1991: first Jewish wedding allowed by law

sure to racist taunts was augmented by the awareness that one was denying and repressing a barely known heritage.

Under *glasnost'*, rumours of impending pogroms grew rife. In this, 'the era of belated confessions, accusations, self flagellations and words... words... words... unimaginably candid, repentant, terrible and superficial', the ideological concern with class was transformed into a passion for tracing national pedigree. There is a tradition among Russian nationalists that gives an almost metaphysical character to the revolutionary incursion into Russian history, and that identifies it with a conspiracy of Jews and Zionists aided and abetted by anonymous 'cosmopolitans'. In the 1960s, for instance, there circulated in samizdat a document compiled by one A Fetisov that offered an interpretation of world history as a struggle between the forces of order and chaos. Jews personified chaos. They had created dis-

order in Europe for 2,000 years, the story ran, and the regimes of Hitler and Stalin represented a positive Teutonic-Slavic intervention which put an end to all that. Fetisov and his collaborators were bundled off to psychiatric wards in 1968, but their views found considerable support among people looking for an accessible vindication of the failures of Soviet Communism.

In fairness, though, *perestroika's* predicted pogroms failed to take place and these days the incentive for Jews to get away seems economic rather than political. Perhaps Anninsky is right to invoke the common legacy of 200 years of Russian-Jewish cohabitation and the characteristics which these 'two nations in mirror reflection' share. Medieval Muscovy referred to itself as 'Jerusalem' and 'the new Israel'. What is Russia's relationship with the Jewish tradition if not that of a newly proclaimed chosen people towards an older rival? One senses in the pages of *Glas* some of the bitterness of a failed historical mission.

'Jews and Strangers' offers a window on the lost years of Russian and Soviet Jewry, at times giving the Jews an exotic, photogenic image which highlights the distinctiveness of Jewish culture and experience. As an attempt to give a voice to a community so long denied one, this is courageous and salutary. But in that it emphasises the 'otherness' of what is sometimes viewed as a quaint cultural type, it could continue to nourish traditional stereotype and prejudice, despite the best intentions. The inclusion of Osip Mandelstam's eulogy of Jewishness in the visual arts, 'Mikhoels' (unfortunately with no indication of date or context), and Nikolai Leskov's 1882 pamphlet in defence of the Jewish contribution to cultural and economic life, is timely given the moods in contemporary Russia. But the two documents also underline the extent to which the Jewish tradition is still viewed as a remote oddity.

Much of the content makes excellent reading. Vassili Grossman's 1934 story 'The Commissar' tells of the reluctant departure of a female Soviet commissar from the Red Army to a Jewish household to give birth to an unwanted child during the Civil War. Grossman depicts the Jewish environment as a preserver of warmth and domesticity — the only humane constant in a displaced world where experiences of childhood and gender have been neutralised or erased.

More ambivalent and puzzling is Leonid Latynin's portrayal of a timeless sequence of attraction and repulsion between Russian and Jew in the excerpt from the second volume of his novel *Sleeper at Harvest Time*.

There is an excellent, sharply drawn vignette by Nina Sadur depicting an episode in the life of the Rosenfelds — a big, sprawling family, nervous, gesticulating, swamped by 'streams of feeling'. They plan to leave for Israel and, to 'outwit the USSR', buy four diamonds to smuggle out of the country. Subsequently, they are robbed and systematically tortured in their own apartment.

To be an outsider is to know oneself to be morally reprehensible. It is to be deprived of the protective shield of self-esteem, to have no rights other than survival and procreation and, perhaps, shy aspirations to self-improvement which will remain unrecognised. In a society and a tradition where the communal experience is all important, it is the greatest transgression of all.

100,000th Soviet Jew arrives in Israel

SOUTH AFRICA

NADINE GORDIMER

Standing in the queue

Is there any South African for whom this day will be remembered by any event, even the most personal, above its glowing significance as the day on which we voted? Even for whites, all of whom have had the vote since they were eighteen, this was the *first time*. This was my overwhelming sense of the day: the other elections, with their farcical show of a democratic procedure restricted to whites (and, later, to everyone but the black majority), had no meaning for any of us *as South Africans*: only as a hegemony of the skin.

Standing in the queue this morning, I was aware of a sense of silent bonding. Businessmen in their jogging outfits, nurses in uniform (two, near me, still wearing the plastic mob-caps that cover their hair in the cloistered asepsis of the operating theatre), women in their Zionist Church outfits, white women and black women who shared the mothering of white and black children winding about their legs, people who had brought folding stools to support their patient old bones, night watchmen just off duty, girl students tossing long hair the way horses switch their tails — here we all were as we have never been. We have stood in line in banks and post offices together, yes, since the desegregation of public places; but until this day there was always the unseen difference between us, far more decisive than the different colours of our skins: some of us had the right that is the basis of all rights, the symbolic X, the

CARLOS REYES-MANZO/ANDES PRESS AGENCY

Orlando West, Soweto, 27 April 1994: for the first time

sign of a touch on the controls of polity, the mark of citizenship, and others did not. But today we stood on new ground.

The abstract term 'equality' took on materiality as we moved towards the church hall polling station and the simple act, the drawing of an X, that ended over three centuries of privilege for some, deprivation of human dignity for others.

The first signature of the illiterate is the X. Before that there was only the thumb-print, the skin-impression of the powerless. I realised this with something like awe when, assigned by my local branch of the African National Congress to monitor procedures at a polling booth, I encountered black people who could not read or write. A member of the Independent Electoral Commission would guide them through what took on the solemnity of a ritual: tattered identity document presented, hands outstretched under the ultra violet light, hands sprayed with invisible ink, and meticulously folded ballot paper — a missive ready to be despatched for the future — placed in those hands. Then an uncertain few steps towards a booth, accompanied by the IEC person and one of the party agents to make sure that when the voter said which party he or she wished to vote for the X would be placed in the appropriate square. Several times I was that party agent and witnessed a man or woman giving this signature to citizenship. A strange moment: the first time man scratched the mark of his identity, the conscious proof of his existence, on a stone must have been rather like this.

Of course nearby in city streets there were still destitute black children sniffing glue as the only substitute for nourishment and care; there were homeless families existing in rigged-up shelters in the crannies of the city. The law places the gown of equality underfoot; it did not feed the hungry or put up a roof over the head of the homeless, today, but it changed the base on which South African society was for so long built. The poor are still there, round the corner. But they are not The Outcast. They can no longer be decreed to be forcibly removed, deprived of land, and of the opportunity to change their lives. They *count*. The meaning of the counting of the vote, whoever wins the majority, is this, and not just the calculation of the contents of ballot boxes.

If to be alive on this day was not Wordsworth's 'very heaven' for those who have been crushed to the level of wretchedness by the decades of apartheid and the other structures of racism that preceded it, if they could not experience the euphoria I shared, standing in line, to be living at this hour has been extraordinary. The day has been captured for me by the men and women who couldn't read or write, but underwrote it, at last, with their kind of signature. May it be the seal on the end of illiteracy, of the pain of imposed ignorance, of the deprivation of the fullness of life.

© *Nadine Gordimer 1994*

ADEWALE MAJA-PEARCE

Left-overs and non-people

Consider the following story. It is the dark days of apartheid. Nelson Mandela is in prison, the African National Congress (ANC) is a banned organisation full of Communist terrorists, and the National Party (NP), in power since 1948, is destined to rule for a thousand years. One Sunday, somewhere in the rural hinterland of the Western Cape province, a neatly dressed coloured man, a Bible under his arm, is walking along the road. His journey takes him past the front gate of a white man, a farmer, who is sitting on his porch contemplating the vineyards that stretch out before him as far as the eye can see. The white man spies the coloured man and calls him over. The following conversation ensues in Afrikaans, the primary language of these parts.

'What is that book you are carrying?'

'A Bible, baas.'

'Can you read?'

'Yes, baas.'

The farmer takes the Good Book and opens it at random.

'What does this say?'

'The Gospel According to St John, baas.'

'Tell me, was this John a white man or what?'

'A white man, baas.'

'So how must you call him?'

'Baas John, baas.'

'Good, now I know that you can read.'

This story was told me by a coloured man in Cape Town, the cousin of a friend, who laughed at the recollection. It was a good story to tell, not least because it captured the sheer banality of a system which purported to rest on an idea — 'something you can set up, and bow down before, and offer sacrifice to' — but was really just a sentimental pretence, proof of which was the speed with which it collapsed, and which, having collapsed, lent itself so easily to ridicule, even (or especially) by those who were its victims.

It goes without saying that my friend's cousin knew perfectly well that a sentimental pretence, in distorting the truth about human relations, can and does destroy lives. He himself had grown up in District Six.

Suddenly, in 1966, District Six was declared a white area and razed to the ground. To illustrate the barbarity of what this meant he took me there. We hadn't gone far from the city centre when he pointed to a huge piece of waste land at the foot of Table Mountain, the cloud-capped landmark for which the city is justly renowned. Looking at the beauty of the setting, to say nothing of its proximity to the centre (shops, offices, theatres), it was easy enough to understand why the architects of apartheid, then under the leadership of the fanatical President Verwoerd (soon to be assassinated by a coloured messenger in the House of Assembly, the very seat of power), wanted it for their own kind; and yet, having done the dirty deed, they were unable to enjoy their newly-acquired real estate because (let it be said) the liberal, English-speaking whites, who happened to outnumber the *boere* in Cape Town, refused to collaborate in a clear case of theft. In the meantime, all sixty thousand men, women and children for whom this was home were relocated to purpose-built townships several kilometres away.

'Look at it,' he said, as we entered one of the townships, 'this is what they thought of human beings.'

We drove for perhaps half-an-hour. Every street we turned into was exactly like the one we had left behind: row upon row of identical wooden boxes on either side of the narrow street with nothing to relieve the monotony, not a single object of beauty anywhere in sight. But there was more to it than the inevitable ugliness of structures erected out of a notion of human life — however 'other' — dictated according to 'the bare scheme of contingent utility' as Hazlitt said, which stamps all such structures with the spiritual emptiness of their creators.

'And then they wonder why the crime rate is so high,' he said, his outrage still palpable more than two decades later. 'Those people were sick,' he added, a conclusion it was difficult to disagree with.

'So you're going to vote for the ANC,' I said when we returned to my hotel room.

He laughed. 'I'm going to vote for the Nats.' He was silent for a moment. 'What happened in the past is over,' he said; 'we have to think about the future now. And I don't trust the blacks. Power will go to their heads, just like it's done elsewhere in the continent. Look at Rwanda, 100,000 dead in the space of two weeks.' He was silent for a moment. 'No, man,' he continued, 'we already know that the ANC will win, which means that we'll need a credible opposition. Only the National Party can provide that. Besides, the *boere* has proved that he can run a modern economy. Why else have so many Africans from the neighbouring countries migrated here in search of work?'

It would have been difficult to refute his argument, even if I had wanted to. Nor did he need to single out the dramatic example of Rwanda, which was then very much in the news. Thirty years of corruption and incompetence had turned one country after another into a disaster zone; worse yet, the levels of sophistry responsible for the mess in the first place were still very much in evidence. So, for instance, the spectacle of a military government, in this case Nigeria, despatching a group of observers to monitor the birth of democracy in the former pariah state barely one year after the Generals had seen fit to subvert the democratic process within their own borders. This went beyond hypocrisy or temerity or plain bad manners to something altogether more sinister, and more deadly. In the meantime, it wasn't even necessary for those same Generals to pass a Group Areas Act in order to clear slums in choice areas for their own benefit, in itself a variation of the apartheid they otherwise loudly proclaimed to be the preserve of others. My friend's cousin needn't have worried on my account. I knew exactly what he was driving at.

'Do other coloured people here feel the same way as you?' I asked him. 'Definitely,' he said; 'the Nats will win in the Western Cape, no question.' 'But people say that this is because the coloureds are racists.' He laughed. 'That's what people always say about the coloureds, and it's true in some cases, especially among the older ones. But the majority are not racists, only... ' He shrugged. 'I don't know how to put it; all I know is that we coloureds have to protect ourselves.'

Nobody doubts that racists are to be found among the coloured community of South Africa, or that the victory of the National Party in the Western Cape was due in some part to the prejudices of the majority coloured population (four out of every seven) for whom a black, ANC-led government was anathema. Almost half a century of apartheid had already provided the insulted and injured with the language in which they could attempt to recover something of their own sense of self-worth, however misguided or deplorable one might judge that to be; but any deeper understanding of what took place among a community which might otherwise have been expected to reject the standard-bearers of apartheid would have to go a good deal further than such a crudely simplistic analysis.

So it was that any number of political commentators, anxious to wag the disapproving finger at the waywardness of their coloured brethren, imagined that it was enough to visit the most deprived communities they hoped they could safely enter in order to hold up to public ridicule the culprits that would prove their thesis. The most vituperative of them, a black journalist with *The Weekly Mail & Guardian*, discovered what he was looking for in the Cape Flats, a notorious township on the edge of Cape Town that even coloured people avoided if they possibly could, and for good reason.

'This is territory where the word *kaffir* is bandied about more liberally than in ultra-conservative Ventersdorp,' the journalist tells us in the course of his article, ('In the coloured Cape Flats, Mandela's just a *kaffir*'), and then proceeds to parade the evidence in the form of two women whose testimony is made to represent the sins of all, as follows:

> [One] resident said she would never vote for Mandela because the next thing the blacks would want to marry her daughters. She would never allow that to happen because '*julle mense het te groot dinges* (you people have things that are too big).' The question of size, she further

volunteered, was the reason she would not sleep with me.

And the second:

> Annetta, a resident who said she was forcibly removed from District
> Six by the *boere*, admitted dislike for Hendrik Verwoerd and BJ
> Vorster because 'they were terrible men', but said De Klerk is the man
> who can be trusted to protect the coloureds from the blacks. 'You see,'
> she explained, saliva spraying through a gap between her front teeth,
> 'we cannot vote for the blacks. Blacks cannot rule. Look what hap-
> pened in Bophuthatswana. And you can't trust the coloureds either,
> *hulle is almal skelms* (they are all rascals).'

The writer's evident lack of empathy for the objects of his scorn —
including, above all, his unnecessary, vulgar and probably fictitious asides
concerning the moral looseness of the one and the unfortunate trait of
the other — renders meaningless any attempt to respond in kind. Such
response as he might reasonably have hoped to generate would necessitate
an equally distasteful attack on flesh-and-blood human beings, at the
same time as it would unwittingly betray personal neuroses — an
appalling sexual vanity, for instance — that is the inevitable consequence
of such dishonesty.

More pertinent again is the way that the article itself mimics the central dilemma of the coloured community, which is their ambiguous status
within the terms of a society based solely on the mythology of colour. A
more intelligent (and certainly less egotistical) journalist with a genuine
concern for the truth of the matter would have understood as much even
as he himself quotes the evidence for this:

> ANC branches in the coloured townships have been hard at work dis-
> tributing copies of a Marike de Klerk interview in which she called
> coloureds 'non-people' and 'left-overs', but this has been to no avail.
> Most residents refuse to make the connection between Marike and
> FW de Klerk.

In one sense, of course, the wife of the last white president is absolutely right, since the coloured, in terms of the apartheid ideology, is defined in the negative; that is, neither black nor white. At the same time, the coloured is absolutely central to the scheme of things, since the definition of human beings as black and white can only make sense in terms of those who occupy the space between the two extremes; that is, coloured.

The coloured, in other words, who is at once victim and symbol of the unspeakable lie, is condemned to exist in a perpetual limbo in order that the mythology of colour might achieve its nightmare reality, the problem being that those who confine them there — who, indeed, need to keep them there for reasons which they themselves are reluctant

SVEN SIMON/CAMERA PRESS

Johannesburg 1985: the mythology of colour

to examine — must then live with knowledge of what they have done. This is as true for the blacks as it is for the whites; but the fact that the former can claim to have themselves been the victims (and therefore innocent) of, say, the Group Areas Act, is the unspoken justification for the unseemly spectacle of a black journalist venting his misdirected rage against those he could have no conceivable argument against.

The coloured, in short, is a fatally easy target, which is why it never occurred to our bright boy to go among the dispossessed whites and ask them why they, in turn, were preparing to vote for the extremist Conservative Party out of a similar mixture of ignorance, fear and a species of self-loathing (at least I'm not black) — one of the more tragic legacies of the apartheid experiment. That he doesn't see fit to do so, if only for the sake of balance, objectivity, journalistic integrity (call it what you like) is because he already knows the answer, just as he knows — or should — that such an article would hardly be of interest to the predominantly liberal white readership of the newspaper for which he works.

That *The Weekly Mail & Guardian* saw fit to publish his scurrilous article, even allowing for the right to reply in the following week's issue — '[The] characterisation of our people in the Western Cape as "rowdy, drunken crowds of NP supporters" can only be rejected with contempt as a supreme insult to the coloured nation' — could only be calculated to confirm what the coloureds already knew about their ambiguous status within the terms of a society in which anybody was free to make statements concerning their attitudes and beliefs, and to do so with an impunity that would otherwise be recognised for the insult it was but for the fact that it reflected and defined the very ambiguity of their position in the first place. It also raised the suspicion, inescapable under the circumstances, that these same liberal whites, who were also witnesses to the unfolding carnage in Rwanda, were just as apprehensive as the coloureds at the prospect of a triumphant black government, the difference being that the coloureds, unlike the whites (or the blacks for that matter), knew a sentimental pretence for what it was; and knew, therefore, the price that might be exacted in the post-apartheid dispensation, if only because their continued survival depended on it.

'We have to think about the future now,' my friend's cousin said to me, and it was entirely significant (but hardly surprising) that it took a coloured to see beyond the euphoria attendant on the forthcoming elections. Half a century and more of a debilitating history is not undone by merely swapping a white face for a black one, as the rest of the continent has already discovered, although the rest of the continent might have fared better but for the absence of a sceptical minority in their midst. Which is why the people of South Africa — *all* the people of South Africa: black, white and in-between — might yet have cause to be grateful that the coloureds in the Western Cape voted as they did. If so, there is a final irony in the fact that such a role should be thrust on those who can be so casually dismissed as left-overs and non-people, but whose presumed marginality turns out to be not so marginal after all; turns out, in fact, to be absolutely central.

DIARY

JON SNOW

On the road

Saturday, 23 April

Five thirty am. Not another vehicle on the road and Cyprien our driver is hurtling along at 20 miles an hour beyond what this VW truck is capable of. But at least you cover 150 in under two hours. Wolmaransstad, when we arrive, is very white, very flat; and deserted. Only later do we discover that this is one of a handful of self-declared white Volkstaats — small enclaves where the white inhabitants somehow propose to live out a separatist existence without consulting the black people who live among them.

In fact, most of the black people live a mile out on a bleak hillside in corrugated shacks. No electricity, an occasional stand pipe but plenty of people. Yet on close inspection, each yard around a shack has been swept and any tuft of grass trimmed.

We have come to find Winnie Mandela. She has been running a remarkable campaign among the shanty squats, reaching out to the dispossessed and the alienated youth. She's already arrived, further up the hill. Somewhere near the top, distorted loudspeakers and a vast throng of people craning to hear. The distortion is peppered with cheers and a forest of fists flung in the air. There's no sign of any media, just two body guards and a woman who travels with her. Close up, Winnie retains the most beautiful countenance. She doesn't want to talk as she leaves, but she does anyway. 'If I don't deliver, they must come and drag me out of Parliament, and I will lead them to the President's door'. She's a vital element in the equation that must form the new South Africa. You think of

Stompe and his murder, with which her 'football team' was charged. You think of her, and the internal exile she suffered; the lonely years in which she was banned from associating with more than one person at any time; of her smashed life with Nelson. Guilt and wounds that bind and divide her and so many others, and which have to be healed if the new beginning is to stand a chance.

Sunday, 24 April
On the road again this time to Brits, near Pretoria, to observe a rally of the white separatist AWB. Five thousand, they say, will turn out. A Wimpy Bar breakfast is rudely interrupted by a gaggle of khaki-shorted men with scars and the occasional amputated limb. They are AWB. One avoids eye contact; they hate the press.

The rally, at a football field mercifully out of town, is sparsely attended — 300 at the most. And Eugene Terreblanche, bearded, deep-voiced and overweight. It is a leadership line-up of old men. Four Belgian nationalist skin-heads with tattooed arms do not mingle easily. There's an air both of menace and absurdity. The right wing bombing campaign has just begun around Jo'burg, but it's hard to imagine these guys have done it. I find myself having to hang onto Terreblanche's puffy hand as I lead him from the stage to our camera. 'I don't encourage the right wing violence,' he says, 'I understand it, and there will be more and more and more.'

Monday 25, April
Back in Johannesburg, I heard the bomb blast half way across town. Desperate damage in and around an ANC regional office, bodies in the street, shards of glass cascading onto the side walks. It had been the biggest blast ever to hit the city. Thabo Mbeki came out to speak for the government-in-waiting. The ANC's press people said he'd do an interview with me on the 20th floor of the Carlton hotel in the early evening.

I used to know Thabo well, last seen in the old Bertorelli's eating spaghetti in London's Charlotte Street. But maybe now things would all be different and he would hardly remember me. After all he would soon be Vice President. He stepped out of the lift, removed his pipe and grinned, and it was if nothing had changed. I had been charged with delivering him the first edition of the new *Index*. He put it in his bag and we talked of respect for the rule of law, and how the ANC would relate to the once whites-only police force.

There's no vindictiveness in these people. They are constantly looking forward, rarely back — soft spoken and constructive, as if the moment of victory is enough to purge the anger and resentment of all apartheid's crime and injustice.

CARLOS REYES-MANZO/ANDES PRESS AGENCY

Ladysmith rally 1994: Mandela and the future

Tuesday, 26 April
Great news! De Klerk's going to talk to us. But the greatest news, the voting is under way — even if in all too many places there are no ballot papers or boxes. The scenes are incredible. In the suburbs of Pretoria, white women with their old black retainers, standing in line, levelled upward by the shared process — talking with each other for longer, and about more, than they had ever talked before. One white liberal woman told me later of her pride at having found herself voting ANC despite earlier misgivings. She had asked her maid of 24 years how she had voted. 'Why, for Mr De Klerk M'am!'

The State President was still at Union Buildings — this Smutsian colonial pile, full of white resonances. I had expected packing cases, a sense of transition. There was none. We set up on the balcony outside his office overlooking palmy gardens and roses. The old orange and blue flag was still up the mast. Here was a man in his final hours of virtually absolute power, about to relinquish it. Yet FW showed no sign of accepting terminal change. In interview he was revealing, certain that he would come back at the next election. 'What do you call Mandela when you call him up in the heat of a crisis?' ' Oh, it's a very formal relationship — I call him Mr Mandela, he calls me Mr State President'. 'D'you like him?' 'I like bits about him, but then again there are things I do not like.'

I left thinking what an ideal man Thabo would be to serve with him as joint Vice President — as indeed it has turned out. De Klerk had no 'road to Damascus'. He was candid: he told me he just realised that apartheid simply had not worked and must go. No great apology for the killing, the jailing, the torture, the sensory deprivation, the censorship. Just, 'it did not work, it was unsuccessful'. I felt another copy of *Index* probably wouldn't go down well. We sipped tea before he left to vote with his 90-year-old mother.

Wednesday, 27 April

More remarkable voting scenes, more ballot box chaos. Tonight Joe Slovo, head of the South African Communist Party, will come on to our programme live. Some hours earlier, Pik Botha's office rings. We've been asking for the foreign minister daily, to no avail. Yes, he'll come too. Should we tell him about Joe? He'll be apoplectic!

Ten minutes to air — Joe's here on the roof of SABC. Pik arrives, sees two chairs and Joe in one. He doesn't want to sit in the other. We talk him into it, as long as they don't have to to talk together once we are 'on air'. I start talking with Joe about reconciliation. Then to Pik, about reconciliation. Then I ask Joe how he can possibly expect to work with a man whose administration killed Joe's wife, Ruth First, in a bomb explosion in Maputo, Mozambique. 'We can't live on in the past: the wound will never heal, it will always be there, but if we are to work this country we have to look forward not back'. I turned to Pik. 'Do you apologise to Joe Slovo?' 'I do. I regret what happened'.

Thursday, 28 April

Six am. Mandela has been up an hour and a half, as per his still-lived prison regime. We have been chosen to conduct one of the few interviews with him over the voting period. They are voting still today. We are back at the ritzy Carlton, back on the 20th floor, waiting for him to come. Appalling failures in the distribution of ballot boxes and papers have continued and he's been hastily summoned to the Independent Electoral Commission to help resolve it.

At eight he comes in, smiling from ear to ear. He recognises Judy our correspondent, Themba our Sowetan soundman whom he treats like a son. I have only met him across the satellite links from London. Charming, charismatic and never 75 — maybe 58ish? He has big strong hands and a firm grip as he greets you. We start, and he unleashes an uncharacteristic fusillade of anger: there has been 'massive electoral fraud' he says. But that off his chest, he returns to the theme Thabo, Joe and Pik had stressed throughout the week: 'let bygones be bygones'. Half an hour later, that handshake again, and being in the presence of one of the great figures of the 20th century had gone. Forget the dispassionate journalist: the prisoner had become a President, and I had been allowed to talk with him.

To Adelaide Tambo for lunch... a wonderful gathering of the great campaigners. Walter and Albertina Sizulu, Mary Benson, Nadine Gordimer, Anthony Sampson and many, many more. A marquee in the garden, a band in the porch and even the most seasoned amongst us can't quite believe that it really has happened. South Africa is free!

Friday, 29 April

The last day of voting. Tonight we shall have Rolf Meyer, the *ancien régime*'s key negotiator, and Desmond Tutu. His leap and yelp for joy upon voting perhaps sums up the cathartic moment that the process became. The lonely crusader of the 1970s and early '80s come home to freedom. Yesterday when I gave Mandela his copy of *Index* he said 'keep an eye on us'. We shall, in hope and expectation of a better life for all. Later, on the long flight north, I dared to hope that the virus of forgiveness and high aspiration hatched in South Africa would somehow eventually affect us all, North and South.

BABEL

PENELOPE FARMER

'We just have to wait and see'

In March this year I spent two weeks in South Africa, accompanying my husband to a neurological conference. It gave me the chance to talk to people about the election, then a month away.

The medical world, for me, was easy pickings. With a Black Sash worker I also visited the Cape Flats townships, and squatter camps like Crossroads. I sat in on Black Sash and ANC advice offices. I spent 24 hours on the overnight train between Capetown and Johannesburg, talking to Afrikaaners. I attended the opening of a recycling project in Soweto and an ANC committee meeting in Johannesburg.

Returning to my notes, I'm immediately struck by the universal apprehension concerning the violence that most had encountered, and all expected to increase, hugely, over the election. Some of the euphoria since may be simple relief that, instead, it decreased. The appalling conditions I recorded in the townships were as expected. Less expected were the green shoots, signs of hope, springing up everywhere in these barren, wind-swept legacies of apartheid. Newly-made gardens; grazing animals; emergent businesses, most utterly basic — piles of bricks, iron, wood, for recycling. It's very small scale still — anything could blight the green shoots. But it's there, waiting for support and encouragement. Let the people speak for themselves.

★★★

Gladys Sithole, hospital worker, Capetown. Mr De Klerk says vote for me, I'm going to build a house for you. People think maybe — but why didn't Mr De Klerk make this before? And now Mr Mandela is pushing. Mr Mandela is our Moses leading the people.

Ingrid Daniels, director SANEL (epilepsy charity), Cape Town. What has happened really? A few boards saying 'Whites Only' have been taken down. In some ways things are worse. People in the rural areas are starving. The ANC has gone out and told people that it's all going to take time. But if you haven't got bread on the table you haven't *got* time.
Lungi, nutritionist, Health Project, Khyelitsha. I'm not sure about these elections. I have a very gloomy picture. There are so many bad things happening, especially when it comes to women. Black women have no rights. The ANC? Who are they? Before you can know a person you have to live with them. The politicians are so far from the people, they don't address our needs. Meantime it's women have to look after the children. Unemployment is the worst thing; it breaks up marriages, puts children in the streets, stops them going to school. Families here are so broken it's unreal. Eight hundred mothers come in here each day for mealie meal and milk to give their children..

Mavis, Breast Cancer Patient, Hillbrow Hospital, Johannesburg. This election? — I don't know anything. I can't read. I need someone to tell me if this person is good to vote for or that one. I don't care if they're Xhosa or Zulu. They must just be good people. Mandela? I don't know him, I don't know any of them. They're just talk talk talk. Peace in my land is all I wish for. I can't hope. I wish. For my kids, my grandchildren.

Lungi. The government is not existing for the moment. As for the violence — if people are hungry, if they have no jobs, of course there will be violence. It's always children who stone the buses. They come back from school and there is nothing else for them to do. In the end, if things go wrong we're the ones going to suffer, not the whites.

Hospital Administrator, Baragwanath Hospital, Soweto. You think there's a lot of people in casualty now? You should see it on Saturday nights. Even our orderly knows that if someone comes in with a knife sticking in their heart, to leave it there. Of course in the last few years, it's been gunshot wounds increasingly, instead of knives.

Gladys. I'm not afraid of the violence if I've got something to defend myself. But the fight isn't finished here. With white people, the mother has a gun, the father has, the baby has a gun even. But we haven't anyone to protect us.

P. Gtolo, hospital cleaner. I am taking a note of your face, and you are taking a note of my face. After all you've got lungs, I've got lungs. You've got a brain. I've got a brain. And maybe tomorrow, you'll be interested in going to my house. But because of the violence you cannot go to my house. So maybe, after the election, the violence is stopped and you can go freely. We can take one another to be brother and sister...

Mavis. If you're with white people from tender age you understand them. But this fighting now — it is all the time. I saw them running riots in Kempton Park last year. I'll never forget it. Boys, girls, all of them were doing it. But not in my house — I have a brick wall and gate and I lock it. I pray for this fight to get finished.

Catherine, aged 29, leukaemia patient, Hillbrow Hospital. The violence is because of apartheid. If white and black people learn to live together, all will be well. I like Mr Mandela. I think he will banish all these past things. Homes, jobs, they doesn't happen so quickly. But just go straight, go your own way, and I think everything goes fine.

Sister Maria, Hillbrow Hospital. People have got to address their differences. They've got to compromise. You're staying with your husband. And you have to make compromises so that you can live with each other. With my people, the Zulus, it's a cultural thing. They see their problems solved at the point of violence. Fighting is normal, like playing, like eating. They don't sit down, negotiate, come to an agreement. And because we were always kept separate none of us understand one another.

Nandi, social worker, Cape Flats. Prejudice is taught white children by their parents and that takes a long time to unlearn. And it won't be easy for any of us to change that. I mean you'll have problems coming to live in my area. But mine will be as bad, coming to live in yours. In my community we hold all-night parties, and no-one would think about complaining. And how are we going to hold our initiations in a white area? Also we'll have to have ceremonies to explain our new life to our ancestors, otherwise we will be quite cut off from them.

Cape coloured nurse, Cape Town. Blacks, whites and coloureds — we're friendly enough on the wards. But outside work we never go to each other's houses. And there's a lot of prejudice. If an inexperienced black nurse does something wrong it's because she's black, not because she's inexperienced.

Norma, Black Sash administrator, Xhosa. Well, me I have a problem with Cape coloureds. I remember a coloured man coming here, into this office, and we asked, how can we help you? But he said nothing, he just looked at us. And in the end he said 'I have never seen a black face in an office. I think I am dreaming. That's why I can't talk.'

Samantha, clinical technologist. Most coloureds support the National Party — it's a matter of 'the devil you know.' Educated coloureds have more exposure to blacks, so they're more likely to support the ANC. The less educated just go by what they read.

Belinda. Language is the problem. First of all, people don't speak a lot of the African languages. And it takes a long time to say something in English that you would normally say in Xhosa or whatever. So in that way too we are not understanding each other very well. All the same there are changes. A lot more people are getting to know each other now. They used to talk about each other, behind their backs. There's still a lot of tension, a lot of uncertainty, people don't trust what others are saying. But there's more obvious attempts to try to get to know people from other race groups. And people respecting you for what you're thinking.

Lucy. What black and coloured people must learn is not to blame ourselves for the way we are. Because the way society has been designed, the separation is deep-rooted in our hearts and minds, that's why we tend to go for different political parties. There's a lot of fear not only in the whites, but in the coloured communities. In their school books, blacks were always the baddies. Till now education for blacks was never seen as important. But it's the crux.

Sister Maria. At the moment, even if you've got standard ten you've got an inferior education. You feel so inferior. To an extent that you tend to be angry. And as soon as you become angry then you start fighting. At grassroots level some of us can hardly afford a newspaper. So our knowledge is never good. That makes it much harder to erase culture — like the Zulu belief you have to fight other people to get what you want. But heredity can be influenced by environment. Those who have gone to school are much more flexible than those that haven't been exposed to school. Kids from different cultures learn to accomodate each other.

Belinda. Far too often in the past, people were disempowered by the mere fact they didn't know. So by educating them you'll give them more power. The problem is so many black people feel they have the right now to be in a powerful job even if they haven't any qualifications. Education is the root — when someone applies for a job, then you know they are capable of it. I don't believe governments can do much. It's people themselves have to do the work.

Lungi. There should be day schools and classes at the end of the school day for women. After all, women are always there for their husbands and children — if they are educated it helps educate the rest. For you see everything has to start with us, here. The smallest resources could make our community live. If you only empower the people. The women. By education or whatever. We can have women sewing — the old people making school uniforms; carpenters making school desks. Gardens selling vegetables. Brick making for the new houses. Investment — big money — is important. Of course government must build factories but they should also be funding self-help projects.

CARLOS REYES-MANZO/ANDES PRESS AGENCY

Welcome Woods Camp, The Cape: transported from the Ciskei

Ingrid Daniels. The strength of the ANC is that it is community linked. It recognises that you have to have empowerment at all levels. Both for the people and for us in our organisations. And things are changing. Because We have to send the state department a statement of intention for each year. Their subsidy used to be used to control us. But now the control has gone. We can structure our services in any way we want.

Bumper sticker in Soweto. 'Love them all, but trust no-one...'

The seaman's tale

My father bought a place in Athlone, but we were turned out of there when they started settling people in rural areas. Out there the farmers treated people as slaves. They put barbed wire round all the best land. You couldn't plant, couldn't graze cattle or sheep. And if you jumped over their fences into their land they could shoot you. We had to build right in the bush — and when everything was spic and span they kicked us out again.

That was around 1949. Up till then education was equal. But then they started giving us inferior education. I was doing my junior certificate at standard eight, but I was going to have to go back to standard one. So I stopped school. I helped my father as a shoemaker. But they stopped that — we weren't supposed to have a business. And so I joined the Merchant Navy and went to sea. But I didn' t want to do that all my life, so I studied electronics in a correspondence course. The course was still in the 1930s, it was all about valves, and we were in the transistor age by then. I got my diploma all the same. And then I worked in electronics. I was in one firm — when I saw the advert in the paper I went in to apply and they accepted me. But I had to go and register with the Bantu Administration and they said no. That job is not for blacks. My case went up to parliament. My employers' s wife was Black Sash, they gave the Bantu Administration hell, and I got the job. I take my hat off to those ladies.

We all used to live together, black and white. But then they separated us out, bit by bit. Separation causes frictions — causes a lot of problems. And what the white man did too was divide the blacks. He made some of us greedy for money, so they're going to carry on with the Nationalists. If I had a chief I would like to respect him. But these old men — they're corrupt — turning against the ANC they turn the whole country upside down. But me, I've always been ANC — my father was too.

We in the ANC don't stand for Communism. We stand for equal rights. I've seen Communism in Estonia and Russia — people queuing for bread and meat in the snow at four o'clock in the morning. That's not our way of life, we blacks. We're socialists — we believe in helping one another. Most of us are born capitalists. We've got cattle. We've got sheep. We've got agriculture. Free enterprise is good, but it's not the answer alone. The whites suffer — they don't have family support the way we all do. And up to an extent they've indoctrinated our children — they don't have respect for their parents the way we did.

Still, I hope things are going to change for the better. People are expecting things so fast — the government must do something very quick. Put up houses. They must invest in jobs — in manufacture — stop all the gold going out of the country and bring us all together again. It's going to take time — five years should be enough. And then we'll see. My grandchildren will be the ones to benefit from the change. They'll have a better life — when we tell them about our history, our hardships, it will seem like a story to them.

'I wish. For my kids, my grandchildren'

22 YEARS AGO

index
on censorship

NADINE GORDIMER

Apartheid and censorship

Written in 1972 following the South African government's plans to abolish the right of appeal against decisions brought by the State Publications Control Board

Removed from the context of its emotive avatars (protection of virtue, protection from temptation; a super-ego policing the obstreperous national id), censorship is control of communication. Not 'communications', mind, but 'communication', that concept that covers the thoughts set in train by the written or spoken word, as well as the word itself, and that in the final analysis is the process by which men reach out and find each other. We speak of the failure of a human relationship as one in which there is 'no communication'. Control of information is merely one of the functions of censorship; its ultimate purpose as a political weapon of apartheid is to bring about a situation where there is 'no communication' between South Africa and the world of ideas that might cause us to question our way of life here, and 'no communication' within our society between the sections of a people carved up into categories of colour and language. Communication is at once intangible and the ultimate in human integration. So long as the lines are down, there is little likelihood of people finding common cause.

How does censorship work as part of the grand design of apartheid? And how effective has it been? Far more than we realise, I think. Picking up a daily newspaper, one may be reassured — and visitors from abroad are often surprised — to see reporting and open debate on contentious subjects. In fact, there is no 'censorship' as such of newspapers; as the editor of one of them pointed out recently, there is no need, because 'all the censoring the government requires is done by the newspaper staffs themselves and their lawyers. It is called 'complying with the law'. And he concludes: 'The laws which enmesh the press in South Africa have brought us a long way along the path of being told only such things as statecraft would wish us to know'...

As for African newspapers, they are controlled by white interests, and it is surely a measure of how unpublishable, in terms of the press-restrictive laws, African opinion on political issues is, to notice that the names of these papers never even come up in the bitter recriminations heaped by the Government on the 'disloyal' press...

When it comes to literature, and in particular the literature of ideas, there has been precious little tolerance to disguise the repression. Tolerance has operated in one small area only, and provides a curious half-light on the psychology of white supremacy. Literature by black South Africans has been successfully wiped out by censorship and the banning of individuals, at home and in exile. But white writers have been permitted to deal, within strict limits, with the disabilities, suffering, hopes, dreams, even resentments of black people. Are such writings perhaps tolerated because they have upon them the gloss of proxy — in a strange way, although they may indict white supremacy, they can be claimed by it because they speak for the black man, as white supremacy decides for him how he shall live?...

But the final measure of the effects of censorship is too often approached from the point of view of writers rather than readers. After all, writers represent a special-interest group, and a small one; censorship affects them professionally; they may write books that cannot be sold or read. But there are many more readers than writers, and the truth is that censorship so far has affected their interests far more seriously than it does the special ones of writers.

Writers whose works are banned may hope to be read another day, or elsewhere; but a whole generation of South Africans is growing up with areas of the world of ideas closed to them, and without any insight into the lives and aspirations of their fellow countrymen, black or white as the case may be, living on the other side of that net of legislation through which we may all only peer at each other dumbly. A book may be banned under any of the Publications and Entertainment Act's 97 definitions of what is 'undesirable'. The success of censorship must be seen in the completeness with which we are cut off not just from the few books dealing with our own ingrown society, but also from the books which formulate the thinking that is going on all around us, in particular on this continent to which we stake our lives on belonging. All this — intellectual isolation, isolation of ignorance among white people about the inner life of their countrymen of another colour — this is the blunting of human faculties that control of communication is steadily achieving. It is essential to the maintenance of apartheid as a whole. We cannot expect to free ourselves of censorship, to bring life back to our numbed human responses, while apartheid lasts.

From Index on Censorship *autumn/winter 1972 volume 1 no 3/4*

LEGAL: RIGHT TO RETURN

DAVID PETRASEK

People in limbo

I remember a refugee camp in south-western Hungary in August 1992. Several hundred Muslim refugees from Bosnia were housed in an old army barracks. This was the time when the horrors of 'ethnic cleansing' were first splashed all over the front pages, and the London Conference was about to begin. The refugees were mainly from Zvornik, a large town on the west bank of the Drina, just across the river from Serbia. Most had fled or were expelled from the town; many hundreds were put on trains and transported to the Hungarian border. Of course, they wanted the war to end, and after that they wanted to go home. Not home to a Muslim mini-state, or an ethnic canton, not to Tuzla, or Bihac or Srebrenica or Sarajevo — all under the control of the Bosnian Government — but home, to Zvornik and the towns and villages around it.

Despite the endless meetings, conferences and peace plans in the ensuing months, none of those entrusted with solving the conflict insisted on the right of the refugees to return to their homes? One or two of the countless UN resolutions made passing reference to the issue and, whenever there is a particularly egregious breach of the latest cease-fire agreement by the Serbs, the odd European foreign minister can be heard angrily demanding a 'reversal of ethnic cleansing'.

For people in danger, the most crucial thing is to be able to flee to a place of safety, to seek asylum and to find protection there until it is safe to go home. This is what the international system for protecting refugees is all about and keeping borders open and ensuring refugees are not forced back across them is what the UN High Commissioner for Refugees was set up to do. But when refugees flee not as a result of conflict but as the intended consequence of it, other issues come to the fore, notably the right to return.

Under international law, people have a right to return to their own country. In a narrow sense, this means that your government cannot expel you or refuse to re-admit you simply because they disagree with your politics. But it also means that no excuse, even war, can justify the mass deportation of civilians from their territory — a crime for which several Nazis were punished at Nürnburg. It should also mean that governments cannot negotiate away this right by agreeing to transfer populations around as part of a settlement to the conflict. Properly understood, the right to return means that the attachments people have to their homes, their villages and towns — their community —

cannot be arbitrarily severed by forcing them into permanent exile. If respected and supported, this right sends a powerful message to 'ethnic cleansers' all over the world: governments and territory may change, but the people who live in a given spot have an abiding right to do so.

'Population transfer' conjures up images from past European wars: serious men in Versailles or Potsdam poring over maps, drawing new boundaries and shifting ethnic and religious groups around with the stroke of a pen. In those times, the diplomats were only slightly uncomfortable with the thought of uprooting hundreds of thousands of people from their ancestral homes. This was the 'price' of peace. A European system of 'nation states', each nation locked inside 'stable borders', led to a preoccupation with ensuring, insofar as possible, that troublesome minorities were expelled to join their own national group: Greeks from Turkey, Turks from Greece, Germans from Poland and Czechoslovakia.

But who would have thought that government agreements to 'transfer' or 'exchange' minority populations would return to be a dominant feature of European politics? Yet this is precisely what is happening with regard to Bosnia. The mediators and those who appoint them are not talking about the right to return because they decided almost from the beginning that to insist on such a principle would complicate,

perhaps even make impossible, the search for a peace agreement.

In the first months of the war, the Serbs took control of upwards of 70% of the territory and expelled or terrorised into flight hundreds of thousands of Muslims in the areas they captured. The other two parties to the conflict have followed suit in areas under their control, albeit on a much lesser scale. It is clear that one of the few 'principles' guiding the deliberations since then has been that since no-one was able or willing to force the Serbs to give up all of the territory they conquered, it was only a question of determining which percentages were agreeable to everyone. An ethnic partition is inevitable we are told and, since this is the 'solution', there will be no return for those refugees whose homes are in the percentage allotted to a different ethnic group. The 'price' of peace: one million Bosnians, probably more (mostly Muslims, but Serbs and Croats too), who will never see their homes again.

In an age of realpolitik it seems quaint to speak about rights and principles, but it is impossible to accept that fundamental human rights can be sacrificed for peace. There are two reasons for this. The first is that peace — a real, stable and enduring peace — means more than the absence of conflict, and any agreement which legitimized the expulsion of hundreds of thousands of individuals from their homes would simply join the list of other infamous peace agreements that have solved little and done a fair share to create new conflicts. However, the peace-makers will argue that history is not so one-sided, that the expulsion of the Germans at the end of World War II and the exchange of populations between Greece and Turkey in the early 1920s, were, however regrettable, necessary and, with time the wounds have healed.

Have they? The Sudeten Germans are still demanding compensation and have powerful political allies in Germany (including on the extreme right) and the whole question is deeply disturbing to the government in Prague. And is it not the hostility between the Greek and Turkish governments, and the threat of them entering the Balkan war on opposing sides, that so concentrates the minds of European statesmen? Even if the historical record showed that in some situations a population 'transfer' provided a genuine solution, such a transfer in ex-Yugoslavia, legitimised by the international community, would be a green light to extreme nationalists in other parts of the world and a recipe for future instability.

The second reason is that to fall victim to the brutal logic of peace at any price is to do great damage to the whole concept of human rights. Human rights as recognized in international law are held by individuals against governments. The UN was given a role in the international supervision of human rights because governments, on their own, could not be trusted to respect these rights. So when governments argue that it is better to achieve peace now (and put an end to more bloodshed) than to stick to principles like the right to return, that undoubtedly complicate matters, we should answer that the choice is not theirs to make. Only the refugees can decide whether to abandon their right to return home, whether they are willing to pay the price set by the peace-makers. But no-one is consulting them.

Again, the peace-makers will argue that this is hopelessly naive; if one accepts that territorial gains will be recognized, then few, if any, of the Bosnian Muslim refugees will want to return to homes that are now under Serb control. True enough. But the principle is nevertheless important, and governments need to be reminded that fundamental human rights are not negotiable. It is only because governments have expropriated the language of human rights, removed it from ordinary human beings struggling to survive, that we end up with a twisted formula where peace and human rights are set up in opposition to each other. But there is no peace without respect for human rights.

No doubt the refugees from Zvornik still want to go home, and it is not too late for those in charge of the peace negotiations to insist, in the interests of an enduring peace and of a commitment to international law, on their right to do so.

ME AND THE CENSORS

SHERE HITE

They stoop to silence

Censorship by any other name spells silence for those who offend the canons of the establishment, especially if they are women

'So you paint freckles on your face? How do you do that?'

I have just arrived at a key interview to present 400 pages of research to the press. This is the first question.

What would you make of it? Or of an article in a major national newspaper covering 20 years of my work which starts: 'At age 50 Shere Hite tottered down the stairs on remarkably high heels.' This is followed by a discussion of whether or not a woman 'of my age' still has the right to wear anything other than 'practical clothing'.

Sexual harassment at work, I guess — in print. And the reader is left to drown in oceans of information about my persona, all ideas disappearing in an over-examined body description. Date rape.

How harmless is this? All of it has an impact on the attitudes of publishers and reviewers to my work: they read these incessantly body-ized articles (why discuss a woman's ideas when you can discuss her body), assume my ideas are equally trivial, and don't always look further. They 'know' who I am.

Which brings me to censorship. Surely, this trivialization, lamentable as it is, is not censorship. Censorship is political discrimination or punishment of those who have certain views inimical to the establishment, those in power. But wait: this trivialization is evident in the editing of my work over the years. It has affected which books I have been 'allowed' to write, ie, those for which I have obtained contracts. Trivialization also exists when editors try to keep 'the beautiful voices' in my research, while removing my own: by removing my conclusions and comment, they effectively silence me.

The *Hite Report on the Family* is the fourth in a series of Hite Reports. Some retain more of my comment than others. This is a matter of the editor with whom I was working: while some encouraged me to expand my ideas, others cut copy to the bone leaving only the bare research data. The denial that women have anything important to say is inherent in some editors' viewpoints — sexism, I am sure, they would not recognise. As Christine Battersby noted in her brilliant book, *Gender and Genius,* men may be called 'geniuses', women rarely are. Even so, one is always left with the thought: maybe the editors are right, maybe there is nothingprofound nor significant in my words.

Freud, it is believed, made profound comments about the nature of human reality, metaphysical in depth. But when I reflect that I have constructed a completely different map from the same territory traversed by Freud — and based on a vastly bigger sample — I do wonder whether people will be able to hear me beyond the boundaries of 'sex and women's' topics, 'women's relationships' and so on.

Making women's ideas invisible is censorship. Simone de Beauvoir mused from time to time that, without being aligned with Jean Paul Sartre, would 'the canons' see her? Accept her? Margaret Mead did a service to society with her ground-breaking research on Samoa — yet the *New York Times* front page obituary only a few years ago felt it correct to state prominently something to the effect that 'although she was never a scientist, nevertheless...' This would never have been said about a man who achieved what she achieved, namely to put an entirely different culture on the map in the mind of the West. Her work was as 'scientific' as that of any other anthropologist, but what do these labels matter, finally?

The attitudes to women and men which I am fighting in my work are the attitudes which everywhere confound and confront my ability to speak and write freely. Together they converge to form an invisible net, so that my ideas and theories are seen through a filter.

I look up with a start at the interviewer who has asked about the freckles. She is peering at me intently, trying to fathom the secret of the freckles. I wonder what I am doing here. But I answer, since departure would become a news item and even more time wasted by rescheduling .

I stammer something like, 'I haven't got any make-up on at all.' I feel small, as if I were having to justify myself to my mother, not unlike the girls in my book. I offer, 'I guess I've always had them.'

'But why are they only on your cheeks, and not all over your face?'

I cannot answer. Panic. 'Well, maybe it has something to do with the changes in hormones as one grows older.' This seems to be an unwel-

---

Women and love

'Terribly important issues that concern women's lives and health, in particular the emotional, psychological and physical abuse of women, are being obscured and trivialised by the media's assault on Shere Hite's new book *Women and Love*. This is tragic at a time when the cases of Hedda Nussbaum and Charlotte Fedder, among others, are before us. There is a clear need to explore the hidden emotional dynamics between women and men. The attack on Hite's work is part of the current conservative backlash. These attacks are not so much directed against a single woman as they are directed against the rights of women everywhere.'

Barbara Seaman	Phyllis Chessler	Kate Millett
Gloria Steinem	Barbara Ehrenreich	Sybil Shainwald
Ntozake Shange	Naomi Weisstein	Ruby Rohrlich
Florence Rush	Grace Atkinson	*1988*

---

come topic (interviewer is about my age) and the subject is changed.

Is it conceivable that a man would be asked such questions rather than about his work? This is not 'intentional' censorship — but it can be worse than the orthodox form since it operates just as surely — but invisibly — to stop ideas from reaching others. It is not glorified by the noble martyrdom attached to the word 'censorship'.

I am not the only woman to experience this. Hundreds of feminist writers, particularly those with a high profile like Naomi Wolf, Susan

Faludi, Andrea Dworkin, Germaine Greer, most 19th century feminists, any woman who speaks out, have been through it. We are called 'colourful', 'dramatic'; details of our bodies and appearances are hashed and rehashed in the press. Still we write and write, talk and talk, hoping to be heard. Sometimes we are, even through the smokescreen.

When I tried to get my ideas across after publishing the third Hite Report, *Women and Love: a Cultural Revolution in Progress* (1987), I came into such conflict with the US media that 12 feminists formed a defence committee for me. There was a heavy-handed attempt by a journalistic clique to silence me during the height of what Susan Faludi calls the 'backlash' and I wound up leaving the country. I have not returned.

The sort of things that happened around that time ranged from gross harassment by national television networks, physical intimidation and disruption at my lectures, hostile taunts and threats left on my answering machine. The media throughout, with rare exceptions like the syndicated columnist Liz Smith, played an invidious role, distorting reports of functions at which I was speaking, proclaiming my 'sins' on prime time news.

I have just opened my mouth in public again with the publication of the fourth Hite Report, this time on the family. Talking to the media will be part of this. In any democracy today, the media is the 'town hall' in which democratic discourse is conducted.

In 1990 I attended a meeting of the women's committee of PEN in New York. Many women were describing not being able to get or renew publishing contracts. They lamented they did not make big enough profits, saying 'only the real money makers get published now.' I said the financial explanation was not sufficient: every day hundreds of books on obscure topics are published. Further, though my books have made money for publishers, the latter tend to be nervous and do not always accept my projects (unless they are about 'sex'); in the reactionary Reagan-Bush climate, feminist books have trouble for political reasons.

The agenda of many large publishing conglomerates is political as well as financial. Their politics range from not upsetting anyone by publishing only safe books to pushing a particular political agenda. Even books by the likes of Noam Chomsky, Gore Vidal, well known feminist activists, or Salman Rushdie, which are likely to sell well, may find their publication discreetly hampered if they express radical political views.

Formal censorship has been replaced by a more insidious phenomenon You must be alert to it before its mists engulf you. It creeps in gradually, bit by bit. It can be hard to recognise until it has become a problem big enough to stifle writers. A prime example of this was the witch hunts in the USA under Senator Joseph McCarthy in the 1950s, when actors and writers went to jail or lost their livelihood for alleged Communist sympathies.

Censorship today is more subtle, often hidden, frequently bizarre. Manipulation of the media by interest groups and politicians, especially by those associated with the fundamentalist right, is highly skilful. It exerts pressures on editors at influential papers who need invitations to White House lunches. Corporations which own the media need the favours and privileged information that Congress and the White House, or Parliament and the prime minister, can give.

Censorship is further aided by the consolidation of publishing, the press and television into ever fewer hands. With fewer people in control, the range of viewpoints and ideas shrinks, access is denied, dissenting voices go unheard.

Another cause for concern is the growing secrecy and paranoia of editorial and marketing committees. Editorial offices are increasingly protected on the outside by armed security. What goes on inside can be equally guarded. Committees make decisions which must be unanimous if they are to get any further; a single person can blackball a decision. Writers and their agents are frequently unaware of the process or the reasons why a manuscript is rejected. Increasingly, only the safest books will get unanimous approval. New and radical ideas almost never make it .

There was a time when editor and author worked together to produce a work which was then presented for marketing. Now, in many cases, there are endless secret consultations and shapings to which the author is not a party. Is this to maintain the 'corporate image'? To please distributors and the bookstore buyers? Or to keep the shareholders happy?

Media monopolies make nonsense of the term 'free market'. The big media conglomerates have already joined battle to expand their territory further with global ownership as the ultimate prize. They have moved into book publishing, not because it is particularly profitable, but because books play an important part in forming public opinion.

Another cause of decreasing diversity and spontaneity in publishing lies in distribution. Eighty per cent of the bookstores in the USA are owned by two chains. They cut prices to a level with which the independent bookshops cannot compete. Small new presses do not have the distribution networks that can compete in reaching a large audience. Nor do they have the connections and financial ties of the larger publishers with the bookshop chains. Where does all this leave the author?

The final aspect of contemporary publishing can, as every author knows, be the most censorious of all. We are talking about the media. Media distortion, harassment, character assassination and disinformation

---

Growing up under patriarchy

'*The Hite Report on the Family: Growing Up Under Patriarchy* — the latest book by ground-breaking researcher Shere Hite — could be a major contribution to America's ongoing debate over rising divorce rates and 'family values'. Unfortunately, you cannot get a copy of this book in America although it has already been published to favourable reviews in Canada, Australia, Great Britain and Holland. The fact that this work by Shere Hite — who has sold millions of books over the last two decades — is being withheld by the US publisher, suggests that the backlash against feminism is far from over.'

Phyllis Chessler	Barbara Seaman	Ruby Rohrlich
Naomi Weisstein	Barbara Ehrenreich	Karla Jay
Jesse Lemisch	Kate Millett	Andrea Dworkin 1994

---

is another form of censorship and can be almost worse than being ignored by editors and reviewers. A publisher will not go to battle for one unfashionable or unpopular author if it means that others on the list will not be reviewed in the mainstream press.

Censorship can also work in the media through quasi-governmental organisations such as those encouraged by Reagan and Bush and described by Susan Faludi in *Backlash*. They operate as hit squads against groups with ideas they don't like. As Pat Buchanan proclaimed in his pro-fundamentalist, back-to-basics speech at the 1992 Republican National Convention, 'The real enemy we have to defeat now is radical feminism.'

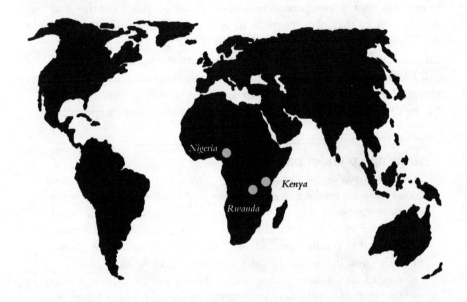

Fear of the dark

Reading the Western press lately, one would think that Africa was composed of just two countries, South Africa and Rwanda. Events there have received widespread coverage; and rightly since those events have been — in sharply different ways — spectacular.

Much of that coverage, of Rwanda in particular, betrays the familiar Western preoccupation with African tribalism. Even in these post-colonial times, the shadow of the Dark Continent of our Victorian forebears still dims our perception of African politics.

When Hutus slaughter Tutsis in Rwanda we throw up our hands in horror, aghast at the barbarism. Such things, we think with a sense of relief, couldn't possibly happen in the civilised North, the tribal slaughter in Bosnia notwithstanding.

This view represents a failure of reason, a failure tainted by prejudice — the fear of the tribal, of the 'primaeval' affiliation by ethnicity that the liberal West thinks to have transcended — that makes any proper understanding of the tensions and conflicts in African politics rationally unapproachable to many Western minds. We, after all, are citizens of nation states. They scarcely more than bushmen, hardly one step away from Hobbes's state of nature.

Just across Lake Victoria from Rwanda, in Kenya's Rift Valley, there is also tribal violence. The Western media have paid scant attention to it, though, partly because it is on a less dramatic scale than Rwanda, partly because much of the province has been closed to outsiders since late last year, precisely to prevent investigation and reporting of the fighting.

Dozens of local journalists have been harassed, detained or arrested for trying to report on the situation there, most prominently the writer and former parliamentarian Koigi wa Wamwere, who is currently in court again.

Wa Wamwere, who founded the National Democratic and Human Rights Organisation (NDEHURIO) has been charged before, with treason and with possessing weapons and seditious publications (that is, NDEHURIO pamphlets). This time he faces the death penalty if found guilty of possessing weapons and attempted robbery.

Wa Wamwere's real offence lies in pushing for true multi-party democracy and an investigation into the ethnic cleansing in the Rift Valley. Human Rights Watch, among others, have found that the Rift Valley violence, which has killed hundreds and displaced hundreds of thousands more, is being stirred up by government forces precisely to prevent political liberalisation and to consolidate the hold on power of President Moi's own Kalenjin group.

So, while there is undoubtedly an ethnic dimension to the violence, succumbing to the facile characterisation of African societies as riven by an irreducible tribalism only plays into the hands of those who would restrict freedom and deny rights. President Moi predicted that a return to multi-party democracy would open the door to tribal bloodletting. And he was right, but it turns out that his was a self-fulfilling prophesy.

In Nigeria, too, where the well-known writer Ken Saro-Wiwa is charged with violent crime, it is the government which commits murder — in this case of the Ogoni people of southern Nigeria, for whom Saro-Wiwa is a spokesman — against those whom they then charge with fomenting tribal hatred.

Some in the West run the risk of falling in too easily with the post-colonial orthodoxy that sees democracy and rights as a kind of neo-colonialism which cannot cope with the 'tribal problem'. But the real risks are run by those like Koigi wa Wamwere who, by struggling for democratic reform and testing their governments' particular form of cultural relativism, are being clearly told: your democracy, your human rights can't work here, and if necessary we will kill you to prove it.

Adam Newey

A censorship chronicle incorporating information from Agence France-Presse (AFP), Amnesty International (AI), the Central American Centre for the Protection of Freedom of Expression (CEPEX), the Committee to Protect Journalists (CPJ), the Canadian Committee to Protect Journalists (CCPJ), the Inter-American Press Association (IAPA), the International Federation of Journalists (IFJ/FIP), the International Federation of Newspaper Publishers (FIEJ), the Media Institute of Southern Africa (MISA), International PEN (PEN), Radio Free Europe/Radio Liberty (RFE/RL), Reporters Sans Frontières (RSF), the BBC Monitoring Service Summary of World Broadcasts (SWB), and other sources.

ALBANIA

It was reported in March that Panajot Zoto, a reporter for the Socialist Party newspaper *Zeri i Popullit*, is in jail awaiting trial for writing an article alleging that the finance minister was involved in importing contraband cigarettes; and that Ilir Keko, of the Social Democratic Party newspaper *Alternative* , was placed under house arrest for making a joke about President Berisha. (CCPJ)

The student newspaper *Reporteri*, banned by Tirana University in November 1993 (*Index* 1&2/1994), resumed publishing at the Media Training Centre in Tirana in March. (CCPJ)

On 3 May President Berisha pardoned Shygyri Meka, and

Koha Jone journalists Martin Leka and Aleksandr Frangaj (*Index* 1&2/1994). Frangaj had been sentenced in absentia on 21 March for divulging state secrets, charges of which he had previously been acquitted. The new trial was initiated after the president publicly condemned the acquittal. (SWB, IFJ)

Former President Ramiz Alia and other former politburo members went on trial on 21 May, charged with abuse of office and violating citizens' rights. Charges against two defendants, Hekuran Isai and Simon Stefani, relate to complicity in the murder of people trying to leave the country in 1990 and to the banning of religious worship and the destruction of religious buildings. (SWB)

On 6 May leaders of the ethnic Greek organisation Omonia were charged with espionage, fomenting separatism, possessing weapons without a licence and maintaining links with the Greek Secret Service. The accused are residents of a part of southern Albania claimed by some Greek nationalists as northern Epirus. Also in May several political parties called for the expulsion of Bishop Anastasios Yannoulatos, Exarch of the Albanian Autocephalous Orthodox Church, after the Greek Embassy in Tirana complained that the Public Order Ministry was trying to prevent Orthodox Easter celebrations. The Albanian Foreign Ministry accused Greek diplomats of 'provocative interference' in the affairs

of the Autocephalous Church. (SWB)

ALGERIA

Journalist Hassan Benaouda was shot dead in the Casbah area of Algiers on 5 March; and Yahia Djamel Benzaghou, who worked for government media including the daily *El Moudjahid*, was shot dead outside his home in Algiers on 19 March. (CPJ, IFJ)

Abdelkader Alloula, a playwright and actor who was shot by unidentified gunmen in Oran, died of his wounds in Paris on 14 March. (*Guardian*)

The offices of the newspaper *L'Hebdo Libéré* were raided by unidentified armed men on 21 March. A photographer, Madjid Yacef, and a driver, Benhaddou Rachid, were killed and three other staff injured. (CPJ)

The newspaper *Alger Républicain* closed down on 12 April. Its printers had refused to continue printing the paper because of outstanding debts which have accrued as a result of non-payment by the state-owned distributors ENAMEP and withdrawal of state advertising. A *fatwa* condemning the paper as forbidden to Muslims was imposed by Islamist groups in 1993. (MENAS Services)

The Ministry of Communication ordered the suspension of the daily paper *L'Indépendant* on 13 April for allegedly 'undermining public order, safety and the higher interests of the state'. (CPJ)

The daily *El Watan* has been threatened with closure by the Ministry of Communication following an article about changes in the presidential administration on 25 May. Editor-in-chief Tayeb Belghiche and the article's author, Khaled Messaoudi, were summoned to the Ministry and threatened with legal action unless Messaoudi revealed his source. (CCPJ)

Ferhat Cherkit of *El Moudjahid* was shot dead by unknown assailants in Algiers on 7 June. The same morning Hichem Guenifi, a technician at Algerian Radio, was also shot dead. (PEN)

ANGOLA

On 5 May Lourenço Agostinho, secretary of the Angolan Human Rights Association (ADHA) was arrested on charges of embezzlement and 'abuse of confidence'. There are concerns that he is being persecuted because of his human rights work. ADHA president and radio journalist William Tonet was also arrested at the end of April and charged with rape. (AI)

Leopold Baio, editor of the daily *Imparcial Fax*, was questioned by police on 19 May and ordered to disclose his sources for a story on police involvement in the corrupt sale of cars. Following Baio's refusal to cooperate, the paper's director, Ricardo De Mello, was also called in. (MISA)

Ric Kinayelako, editor of the opposition party newspaper, *Batuque Amana*, was attacked in his home by people wearing army uniforms around 19 May. (MISA)

BBC and Inter Press Service correspondent Chris Simpson was detained on 12 June after interviewing South Africans held in Luanda on drug trafficking charges. Unconfirmed sources say he may be deported. (MISA)

Recent publication: *Media in Angola — Report of the MISA Task Force to Angola, December 1-8* (MISA, 1994, 16pp)

AZERBAIJAN

Five staff members of the opposition Popular Front newspaper *Azadlig*, Ganimat Zahidov, Hikmet Zeynalov, Rafig Mammadli, Gorkhmaz Ibrahimov and Kanan Salimov, were detained for several hours by police on 18 April. The police were believed to be searching for weapons in the newspaper's offices. (PEN)

BANGLADESH

Rahman Motiur Chowdury, editor of the *Daily Bangla Bazar Patrika* was arrested on 21 April and detained. The arrest warrant was issued in a defamation case filed by the special envoy of the prime minister. Arrest warrants have also been issued against the newspaper's publisher. (PEN)

Threatened writer Taslima Nasreen (*Index* 10/1993) has gone into hiding following the issue of a warrant for her arrest on 4 June on a charge of insulting religious beliefs. The charge arises from an interview she gave to the Indian paper *The Statesman* in May, in which she was quoted as saying that the Quran should be revised. Nasreen, however, says she was misquoted. The police protection provided after Islamist extremists called for her death over her book *Lajja* (Shame) has now been withdrawn. (PEN)

Arrest warrants were issued against four editors of the daily *Jankantha* on 8 June, apparently in connection with an article on a group of religious leaders known as the Fatwahaz. The arrest orders followed a number of demonstrations at the offices of *Jankantha* and another daily, *Bangla Bani*, in which around 15 people were injured by Islamists calling for the papers to be banned and for the execution of Taslima Nasreen (see above). Two of the four editors — Toab Khan and Borhan Ahmad — are detained; Atiqullah Khan Masud and Shamshuddin Ahmad are in hiding. (PEN)

BOSNIA-HERCEGOVINA

Fran Jezidic, correspondent for the Croatian daily *Slobodna Dalmacija*, was reported in late March to be imprisoned near the village of Bugojno. (PEN)

Brian Brinton of the news agency Magnolia News and Francis Tomasic of the New York music magazine *Spin* were killed by a landmine near Mostar on 1 May. Another *Spin* journalist, William Vollmann was seriously injured in the same incident. (PEN)

Associated Press correspondents Misha Slavic and Srdan Ilic, and *Daily Telegraph* reporter Mike Montgomery were ordered to leave Serb-controlled Bosnia in mid-April. (PEN)

Recent publication: *War Crimes in Bosnia-Hercegovina — Bosanski Samac* (Human Rights Watch/Helsinki, April 1994, 19pp)

BRITAIN

Some 200 asylum seekers held at the Campsfield immigration detention centre went on hunger strike in mid-March in protest at their continued detention. Over 650 are being held without being charged with any offence. In May the Council of Europe launched an investigation into whether the practice of detaining asylum seekers constitutes cruel, inhuman or degrading treatment. (*Guardian*)

Telephone tapping and interception of mail by the police, customs and security services have reached their highest level ever, according to official figures released on 31 March. The number of warrants for phone taps, each of which can cover multiple lines, has doubled in the last six years to over 1,000. One commentator estimates that at least 40,000 lines could be under surveillance. (*Sunday Times, Independent, Daily Telegraph*)

Further curbs on videos containing scenes of sex and violence were forced through Parliament by backbench MPs concerned at alleged links between childhood delinquency and screen violence. The government agreed in April to give further powers to film censors and will introduce new warning labels on videos. Britain already has the most restrictive laws on videos in western Europe. (National press)

Up to 10 health publications on sex and HIV-related education are to be withdrawn following pressure from right-wingers within the government who regard them as too explicit, it was announced in April. (*Guardian*)

A BBC television documentary on corruption in a leading Conservative-controlled local council was dropped the day before it was due to be screened on 25 April. The programme accused Conservative members of Westminster Council of gerrymandering, using £50 million of public money. The BBC has denied withdrawing the programme because of political pressure. (*Sunday Times, Observer, Independent*)

Secret wartime documents released in May reveal that Britain blocked a plan to rescue 70,000 Romanian Jews during World War II. The Foreign Office urged the United States to drop the plan as it considered it too difficult to resettle the refugees. (*Sunday Times*)

Recent publication: *Northern Ireland — Continued Abuses by All Sides* (Human Rights Watch/Helsinki, March 1994, 10pp)

BULGARIA

Parliament decided on 21 April to take greater control over the official news agency BTA, including appointing the agency's director. A measure to prevent BTA publishing 'slander or untrue allegations' against the president, Parliament, or other state institutions was also approved. (RFE/RL)

Police used force to prevent an assembly of the Ilinden United Macedonian Organisation (IMRO) at Rozhen Monastery on 24 April. The annual gathering, which commemorates the death of Yarie Sandanski, a prominent figure in the struggle against Ottoman rule, was deemed anti-Bulgarian. Dozens of ethnic Macedonians, including IMRO members, were reportedly beaten by police after attempting to visit the monastery. (SWB)

Bulgarian TV failed in May to abide by a court ruling to reinstate journalist Margita Mihneva, fired in 1993. Television director-general Hacho Bojadgiev has dismissed many well-known journalists since his appointment in 1993, including Sacho Dickov, Petko Georgiev, Ivo Indjev, Lili Marinkova, Nina Selvieva and Ivan Takev. A number of programmes critical of the government, such as *Conflicts*, *Lutch* (Ray), *Zashto* (Why) *Oshte* (Still) and *Ochevidtzi* (Eyewitness) have also been cancelled. (International Press Institute)

On 3 May the government denied allegations made by the Bulgarian Independent Trade Union (CITUB) that the telephones of unionists planning a strike the next day had been tapped. The 4 May rally in Plovdiv was banned but workers held a silent march. Police arrested four union leaders, including CITUB executive secretary Doncho Donchev. It was also reported that workers were prevented from holding a rally in front of the Council of Ministers building in Sofia. (SWB)

The Union of Democratic Forces announced on 30 May that it will set up a commission to check whether the parents of any of its senior members had ever been members of the Communist Party leadership and whether any had themselves applied to join the Communist Party. (SWB)

Five people were injured in a grenade attack on the offices of the newspaper *Antarakom* on 24 March. Police report that two unidentified men hurled the grenade into the offices of the Khmer-language newspaper from a motorcycle. The motive for the attack is unknown. (PEN)

The government submitted a draft press law to the National Assembly on 16 May. If passed, the new law would prevent 'incitement to disrupt public order'; enforce the retraction of statements that damage a person's reputation, whether accurate or not; and impose licensing restrictions on journalists. Official approval would also be required to open a printing centre or bookshop.

Interior ministry forces surrounded the publishing house of the newspaper *Sokal* on 16 May and seized ten thousand copies, along with publishing equipment. The newspaper has since reportedly been closed down for criticising the king, which is prohibited under the new Constitution. The paper had suggested that the king was responsible for more than one million deaths under the Khmer Rouge regime. (RSF)

The independent weekly *Perspectives Hebdo* was suspended on 23 March by the Ministry of Territorial Administration, apparently for not conforming to censorship regulations which require two copies of every issue to be deposited with the authorities before publication. The suspension follows the publication of an article on the marriage of President Paul Biya in the 17 March issue, which had been submitted for prior censorship but which was seized by the police within a few hours of going on sale. (RSF)

The 6 April edition of the newspaper *Le Messager* was banned by the governor of the country's coastal province, Ferdinand Koungou Edima, for 'disturbing public order'. The paper's cover story discussed the tenth anniversary of the failed coup attempt of 1984. This is the fourth time within a month that copies of the newspaper have been seized (*Index* 1&2/1994). (RSF)

Thomas Patrick Eyoum'a Noth, editor-in-chief of the independent weekly *Dikalo*, was interrogated by the police in Douala on 20 April, after publishing an article which linked the names of two ministers with the arrival of a container full of banknotes in Douala on board a ship from Europe. Eyoum'a Noth was questioned about his sources for the story, despite the fact that under Cameroonian law journalists are not obliged to reveal sources. Eyoum'a Noth was further detained and interrogated on 4 May. (RSF)

On 3 May, World Press Freedom Day, the communication minister, Augustin Kontchou Kuoumegni, declared that the government is planning to liberalise the press laws. The press in Cameroon has come under increasing scrutiny by the police and security forces in recent months. (RSF)

CANADA

Charges against painter Eli Langer (*Index* 1&2/1994) were reported to have been dropped in March, but officials are said to be seeking court permission to destroy the paintings seized in a police raid on an exhibition of his works. (Feminists for Free Expression)

In March 16,000 copies of the San Francisco-based computer magazine *Wired* were withdrawn from distribution because they carried a report of a rape and child abuse trial in Toronto, in which the judge has ordered a complete media ban. The magazine was reporting the story as an illustration of how computer users with a modem can circumvent restrictions on information. (*Boston Globe*)

Khalid Abdul Mohammad, a former aide to black nationalist leader Louis Farrakhan, was barred from entering the country on 30 April. He was due to address a black student group at the University of Toronto and immigration officials reportedly feared that he would violate the laws prohibiting hate speech. (*New York Times*)

Paul William Roberts, author of the novel *Palace of Fears*, was stabbed at his home on 12 May

and has since gone into hiding. His publisher, Random House, has received two letters accusing Roberts of blasphemy over the book, which is set in Egypt and contains quotations from the Quran. (*Times*)

CHINA

Hong Kong journalist Xi Yang (*Index* 1&2/1994) was sentenced to 12 years in prison for stealing state secrets on 28 March, following a closed trial in which he was denied legal representation. His co-defendant Tian Ye, a Central Bank clerk, was sentenced to 15 years' imprisonment for supplying information to Xi. The Hong Kong Journalists' Association has denounced the sentences as 'illegal and extremely unreasonable'. A senior Chinese official in Hong Kong, however, has denied that China is trampling on press freedom, saying 'reporting on the mainland is pretty free as long as you don't break the law'. By invoking a state security law to punish Xi, Chinese authorities have heightened concerns that Hong Kong's journalists may suffer severe restrictions on information-gathering after 1997. (*International Herald Tribune*, CPJ, Article 19)

Wei Jingsheng (*Index* 1&2/1994) was detained in April after meeting US official John Shattuck and will reportedly stand trial for treason. If convicted, he could be sentenced to death. (*Daily Telegraph*)

Wang Juntao, one of two 'black hands' behind the 1989

Tiananmen Square protests, was released for medical treatment on 23 April after serving four years and five months of a 13-year sentence. The other, Chen Ziming, was freed in early May, also for medical treatment. (*Independent*)

On 5 May the Popular National Assembly adopted stringent new measures to strengthen the Public Order Law. The amendments create 18 new categories of public order offence, including 'activities in unregistered associations'. (RSF, *International Herald Tribune*)

Ten Hong Kong journalists who were planning to cover the official visit of a Taiwanese delegation to Zhejiang province were prevented from entering the country on 5 May. According to the Xinhua News Agency, the 10 were denied entry because they had condemned the sentencing of Xi Yang. (RSF)

Police in Shanghai prevented the artist Ling Muchen from boarding a flight bound for the US on 6 May. Ling, a member of the local Association for Human Rights, had been given a US study visa. Several days earlier police also detained Li Guotai, chairman of the Association, which is fighting for official registration. (*International Herald Tribune*)

The US President, Bill Clinton, announced on 13 May that China's Most Favoured Nation trade status would be maintained, breaking the link between human rights and trade. He proposed a series of measures intended to maintain at least some pressure on China, including a ban on the import of Chinese weapons and ammunition, the enhancement of Radio Free Asia and Voice of America broadcasts, and increased government support for human rights groups. Clinton argued that the human rights situation in China would be improved by closer relations with the US. (*International Herald Tribune*)

The condition of writer Bao Tong, who was arrested after the Tiananmen Square protests, is deteriorating, it was reported on 23 May. According to his family, he is receiving inadequate medical attention and they believe prison authorities are deliberately denying him access to his medical records. (Human Rights Watch)

On 23 May seven dissidents publicly petitioned the government for a reassessment of the Tiananmen Square massacre and compensation for the families of victims. The group, led by Wang Dan (*Index* 1&2/1994), are all on the most-wanted list of student leaders and have previously been imprisoned for their part in the protests. (*International Herald Tribune*)

A crew from the South Korean television network Mon Hwa Broadcast Company was expelled from China on 27 May for working without authorisation. The four journalists were reportedly working in Jiangsu rather than Shandong province, where they had been scheduled to

report on economic cooperation between China and South Korea. (RSF)

Police detained four members of a news crew from the US network CBS on 3 June, while they were filming in Tiananmen Square. They were released only after signing an apology for breaking certain rules and for filming a policeman. Their video tape was also confiscated. The previous day, the Public Security Ministry ordered major hotels in Beijing to suspend delivery of the US news network CNN, apparently in anticipation of the fifth anniversary of the Tiananmen Square massacre. (RSF, CPJ)

Recent publications: *China: New Arrests Linked to Worker Rights* (Human Rights Watch/Asia, March 1994, 17pp); *China: No Progress on Human Rights* (Human Rights Watch/Asia, May 1994, 46pp); *The Price of Obscurity in China: Revelations About Prisoners Arrested After June 4, 1989* (Human Rights Watch/Asia, May 1994, 51pp); *Human Rights Violations Five Years After*

Tiananmen (Amnesty International, June 1994, 48pp)

COLOMBIA

Four bishops were reported in March to be the subjects of a criminal investigation over alleged links with guerrilla leaders from the National Liberation Army (ELN) and the Colombian Revolutionary Armed Forces (FARC). All have criticised the army for human rights abuses and have advocated peace talks with the rebels. (*Latinamerica Press*)

Horacio Yepes Lozano, columnist with the weekly *El Tabloide* and radio host with the station La Voz de los Robles, was shot dead by a motorcyclist in Tulua on 25 May. Abelardo Marín Pinzón, an editor for the television station Telepacifico, was also killed in Tulua in a similar manner on 27 May. It is unclear whether the incidents are related. (IAPA)

In late May the head of the internal security service threatened to take legal action against Amnesty International over allegations of political murders by the armed forces contained in the report *Political Violence — Myth and Reality*. A British Foreign Office minister, Tristan Garel-Jones, has accused Amnesty of inflating their allegations to raise money. (*Guardian*)

Recent publication: *State of War: Political Violence and Counterinsurgency in Colombia* (Human Rights Watch/Americas, December 1993, 149pp)

PINTER 94   RSF

CONGO

Two Radio Congo journalists, Yves-Roger Yebeka and Marcel Mallet Ombamba, were stopped by police on 10 May after going to Oyo to interview ex-President Sassou-Nguesso on the outcome of the South African election. The recordings they made were confiscated. Yebeka was detained until 14 May, apparently for having state property in his possession and for having left on an assignment without permission. Marcel Mallet Ombaba is also accused of leaving Brazzaville without permission. (RSF)

COSTA RICA

The Journalists' Association commission investigating the case of Pilar Cisneros and Isabel Ovares (*Index* 1&2/1994) ruled in March that the two had conspired to 'broadcast information against the person, honour and candidacy' of President-elect Figueroas. Five other journalists were also censured by the commission. (CEPEX)

Over 30 people were injured, four seriously, when Civil and Rural Guard members used tear gas and rifles to disperse a picket by striking banana workers outside the Geest plantation in Sarapiquí on 13 May. (AI)

COTE D'IVOIRE

On 24 March five journalists with the opposition daily *La Voie* — Abou Dramane Sangare, Freedom Neruda, Jacques Prejean, Cesar Etou and Souleymane Senn — were sentenced to one year in prison for insulting President Bédié (*Index* 1&2/1994). The paper was also fined 200,000 CFA. Sangare and Senn were further sentenced to three years' imprisonment for inciting violence and disturbing public order on 21 April in connection with an article which argued that the opposition could make the country ungovernable through a concerted campaign of strikes, civil disobedience and marches. (PEN)

David Deliwa Gogbe, editor

of the weekly opposition newspaper *Le Changement*, was sentenced to a year in prison on 24 May, having been found guilty of defaming Germain Coffi-Gadeau, a senior government official and close friend of former President Félix Houphouët-Boigny. The charges arose from an article implicating Coffi-Gadeau in criminal activities. (RSF)

CUBA

Video equipment belonging to journalists with the US news programme *MacNeil-Lehrer Newshour* was stolen by three men who claimed to be policemen in Havana on 28 April. The journalists were on their way to interview human rights activist Elizardo Sánchez (*Index* 3/1993). (CPJ)

Poet and journalist Yndamiro Restano Díaz (*Index* 8/1992, 8&9/1993) was reported in May to be still in detention and in poor health. He has served two years of a 10-year sentence for counter-revolutionary propaganda and inciting civil disobedience. (PEN)

Francisco Chaviano González, president of the unofficial National Council for Civil Rights in Cuba (CNDCC), was arrested in Havana on 7 May, reportedly shortly after being handed a compromising document which was used as a pretext for his detention. The homes of five other CNDCC members were raided the same day and files confiscated. (AI)

Recent publication: *Stifling Dissent in the Midst of Crisis* (Human Rights Watch/Americas, February 1994, 11pp)

CYPRUS

Theocaris Theokli Theocharidis, a Jehovah's Witness, was tried in late May for refusing to perform military exercises proscribed by his religion. He faces a possible prison term of between one and five months. (AI)

CZECH REPUBLIC

An Iranian Embassy spokesman stated on 29 March that the Cesty Publishing House's plan to issue a Czech edition of *The Satanic Verses* would compromise the Czech Republic's relations with the Islamic world. The Foreign Ministry said that the State had no place to dictate the business of private publishers. (SWB)

In April the Constitutional Court abolished parts of the criminal code relating to offences of defamation of public officials and political institutions, on the request of

President Havel. However, articles 154 and 156 pertaining to slander of a state organ remain in force, along with provisions against defamation of the Republic and President. (RFE/RL, AI, SWB)

President Havel criticised a Radio and Televison Council decision to give a former Czech Radio frequency to a private operator in April. Czech Radio ceased broadcasting on the frequency in December 1993, reportedly because of economic constraints. (SWB)

Police in Hradec Kralove (East Bohemia) confiscated knives, chains and gas pistols from skinheads arriving in the town on 23 April. The skinheads denied that the purpose of the rally was to celebrate Hitler's birthday. (SWB)

DOMINICAN REPUBLIC

A Foreign Ministry communiqué released on 19 May accused foreign journalists and international election observers of interfering in the country's internal affairs and of promoting unification with Haiti. The document warned journalists of possible curbs on reporting if they were thought to be endangering national security. (CPJ)

Journalist and university lecturer Narciso González has disappeared after reportedly being detained by soldiers on 26 May. Shortly before the 16 May presidential elections González published an article in *La Muralla* magazine entitled 'Ten reasons why [President]

Balaguer is the most perverse figure in the Americas'. He also protested the conduct of the elections, which were allegedly marred by fraud. (AI)

EGYPT

Four journalists at the paper *Al-Sha'ab* (*Index* 1&2/1994) have been detained on charges of 'inciting hatred against the government and threatening social peace and national unity'. Mohammed Helmy Mourad, Mustafa Bakrim, Magdi Hussein and Adel Hussein were questioned in March over articles about the 25 February massacre in Hebron. Another *Al-Sha'ab* journalist, Abdel-Sattar abu-Hussein, was sentenced to one year's imprisonment with hard labour on 30 April as a result of articles containing classified military information. (CCPJ, RSF, Egyptian Organisation for Human Rights)

The 18 March edition of the London-based Arabic newspaper *Al-Hayat* was reportedly banned because of an article about the execution of two Islamist militants found guilty of plotting President Mubarak's assassination. (CCPJ)

Ahmed Ibrahim El-Baradei of the daily *Al-Akhbar* was shot dead on the night of 2-3 April in Qalioub, north of Cairo. (RSF)

In May the Oscar-winning film *Schindler's List* was reportedly banned because it contains scenes of violence and nudity. (*Guardian*)

Publication of the English-language weekly *Middle East Times* was suspended for a week in June on the orders of the government. No reason for the suspension was given. (RSF)

Recent publication: *Prisoners Without Rights* (Egyptian Organisation for Human Rights Field Studies Unit, 1994, 34pp)

EL SALVADOR

Oppostion election candidate Heriberto Galicia was shot dead in San Miguel on 27 March. He had previously received death threats and his colleagues in the National Revolutionary Movement believe the killing was politically motivated. (AI)

FMLN opposition member José Isaías Clazada Mejía was killed in Jicalapa on 24 April after being threatened with death by members of the ruling ARENA party. He was overseeing the elections in his municipality and had reportedly quarrelled with the ARENA members over alleged voting irregularities. (AI)

Recent publication: *Darkening Horizons: Human Rights on the Eve of the March 1994 Elections* (Human Rights Watch/ Americas, March 1994, 20pp)

ESTONIA

On 21 March the board of the paper *Rahva Haal* (People's Voice) voted to dismiss Toomas Leito as editor-in-chief and replace him with Olev Remsu. More than half of the paper's staff signed letters of

resignation and took over the newspaper's publishing. They denounced the government for 'pursuing an unambiguously party-biased policy, disguised as protecting the interests of the state'. (FIEJ)

ETHIOPIA

Tefera Asmare (*Index* 1&2/1994), editor of the weekly *Ethiopis*, was sentenced to two years' imprisonment on 25 March. He had been in detention since November 1993 after publishing one article about ethnic conflict in the Gondar region and another critical of the government. (RSF)

Asrat Damtew, Antensay Tafesse, Tesfaye Berehanu, Kinfe Assefa, Mulugeta Jigo, Nesanet Tesfaye, Mesele Haddis, Kibret Mekonnen, Befekadu Moroda Iskander Negga and Yohannes Abebe (*Index* 1&2/1994) have all been provisionally released. Some are reportedly on bail, having been charged with offences against the 1992 Press Law. (AI)

In March Girma Lemma, editor-in-chief of the weekly

Aphrodyte was sentenced to one year in prison for having published 'articles and photographs which offend public morals'. Izedinn Ali, editor-in-chief of *Yefker Tchawatta* (Love Games) was sentenced to two years on the same charge, having been unable to pay a fine of US$2,000. (RSF)

Other journalists imprisoned because of their inability to pay fines include Kassa Keraga, Daniel Tadesse of *Waqt* (both now released), Tamrat Gibri Georgis of *Tomar* , and Daniel Kifle of *Fendisha* (*Index* 1&2/1994). Girmay Gebre Tsadik, reported to have been imprisoned because he could not pay his rent, has also been released. (RSF, AI)

Meleskachew Amha and Berehane Mewa (*Index* 1&2/1994) of *Dewol* were released on 16 March and immediately rearrested. They have not been charged but are reportedly accused of complicity in the attempted murder of a US citizen. The weekly had published a letter from an unknown armed group which claimed responsibility for an attack on a US embassy official in January. (PEN, AI)

It was reported in April that several newspapers have ceased publication since March as a result of anti-press measures, including the banning of the sale of publications on the streets. The affected publications are: *Muday, Alef, Asmero, Ruh* and *Mahlet* (all monthlies), and the weeklies *Moged, Tomar, Beza* and *Twaf*. (Association of Ethiopians in Holland)

Nayk Kassaye (*Index* 1&2/1994), editor of *Beza* magazine, was released on bail in April but disappeared on 9 May after leaving his parents' home. It is feared that he may have been detained by the security forces. (AI)

FRANCE

In early April the Nazi collaborator Paul Touvier became the first Frenchman to be convicted for crimes against humanity. He was accused of murdering seven Jewish prisoners at Rillieux-la-Pape near Lyons in June 1944. Touvier was twice sentenced to death in absentia after the war, before being pardoned by President Pompidou in 1971. (*European*)

On 14 April the Senate voted in favour of a bill which, if approved by the National Assembly, would ban the use of foreign words in advertising, in public announcements and on radio and television. (*Guardian*)

Zairean journalist Bobo Kunzi-Mutanga was ordered to return to Zaire on 21 April following a rejection of his application for refugee status. According to human rights organisations, he faces imprisonment if he is deported. (RSF)

GABON

On 7 April Yves Jaumain of RSF was expelled from Gabon within a day of his arrival there to investigate recent violations of press freedom, in particular the case of journalist Rostand Vecka Brice Nang of Radio Liberté (*Index* 1&2/1994). Four pages of his notes were taken

from him and photocopied, including telephone numbers and the names of two lawyers close to the political opposition. (RSF)

GAMBIA

Davies Michael Iber (*Index* 1&2/1994), president of the International Society for Human Rights, was not, as previously reported, detained in relation to an article he published in the *Daily Observer*. Rather, he was called in for questioning by the police after members of his own organisation accused him of misappropriating the Society's funds. (*West Africa, Gambian Daily Observer*)

GEORGIA

Zazou Chenguelia, director of the independent television station Ibervisa in Tblisi, was violently beaten on 23 March by six armed men. Station staff had received several threats over a programme which criticised the former defence minister. The station was bombed on 26 March. (PEN)

GERMANY

On 15 April the government decided not to ban the far-right Republican Party, despite clear signs that it has links with neo-Nazi activists. A ban, it was argued, would make martyrs of the party leaders and drive the 23,000 active members underground. (*Times*)

The Justice Ministry drafted a law in May, which would make it an offence to deny that the Holocaust took place. The

Interior Ministry estimates that 8,000 extremists are campaigning to deny German guilt for Nazi atrocities and for an end to German war reparation payments. (*International Herald Tribune*)

The proposed transfer later this year of the Berlin Documentation Centre, which houses Nazi and SS records, has outraged Holocaust scholars who fear that, once the transfer has taken place, information may become inaccessible owing to the strict privacy laws. The federal archive law states that the privacy laws should not apply to serious scholarly research. (*Independent*)

GREECE

In early May the right-wing newspaper *Stohos* published the address in Thessaloniki of Anastasia Karakasidou, a Greek scholar who has conducted research into the Slavic-speaking community in Greek Macedonia. Karakasidou, who has decided not to publish her dissertation on the subject, has already received numerous rape and death threats. On 18 May *Stohos* also published the address of George Nakratzas, who has written on the ethnology of northern Greece. (PEN)

Hristos Sideropoulos, a Macedonian activist living in Greece, is to be tried in June for 'spreading false information'. The government denies the existence of a Macedonian minority and language within Greece. (*Independent*)

Recent publication: *Denying Ethnic Identity — The Macedonians of Greece* (Human Rights Watch/Helsinki, April 1994, 85pp)

GUATEMALA

Five prominent journalists (Gustavo Berganza and Iduvina Hernández of *Crónica*; José Rubén Zamora and Julio Godoy of *Siglo Veintiuno*; and Eduardo Zarco of *Prensa Libre*) received a letter on 22 March, threatening them and their families if they did not leave the country immediately. The letter, purportedly sent by the URNG guerrilla force, accused the five of unfavourable reporting of the URNG. The URNG have denied sending the letters. (CEPEX)

On 14 April Rafael Aragon Ortiz, marketing director of *Prensa Libre*, was abducted by three armed men who forced him to write an article critical of the government and ordered him to publish it in his newspaper. (CEPEX)

A bomb destroyed part of the home of lawyer and *Crónica* editor Fernando Quezada Turuño on 31 May. Quezada believes the attack was not related to his work, but was intended 'to attract publicity or generate terror', possibly in connection with the recent resumption of peace talks between the government and the URNG. (CEPEX)

GUINEA

On 9 March police raided the offices of *Radio Frequence Gandale*, the country's first independent radio station, and closed it down. Employees had to leave the building after the police threatened to destroy equipment. No reason has been given for the closure. (RSF)

HAITI

Independent news media are increasingly constrained by restrictions on reporters' movements, selective self-censorship, disinformation from official sources and political control, according to the Group for Reflection and Action for Liberty of the Press. (Haitian Information Bureau)

Former Radio Soleil journalist Jean Mozart Thibault was detained and severely beaten by soldiers in Thiotte on 13 May. They accused him of distributing 'pamphlets calling for people to rebel against the military government' and tried to extort a ransom for his release. (RSF)

The sister of Haitian-American journalist Jacqueline Thomas was strangled to death in Port-au-Prince on 8 May. Her murder appears to be linked to threats received recently by Thomas, who hosts the programme *Haiti Conscience* on a New York television station, from the pro-army Front for Haitian Progress (FRAPH), which has an office in New York. (Haitian Information Bureau)

Recent publication: *Terror Prevails in Haiti — Human Rights Violations and Failed Diplomacy* (Human Rights Watch/Americas and National Coalition for Haitian Refugees, April 1994, 46pp)

HONDURAS

Several senior officials of the Committee of Relatives of the Disappeared (CODAFEH) received death threats in early March, apparently in response to their pressure for investigations into past human rights abuses. (AI)

A proposed privacy law, which came before Congress in May, has been criticised for failing to distinguish between private individuals and public figures. Journalists fear the law could be used to inhibit reporting on the activities of politicians. (IAPA)

HONG KONG

Chan Ya's regular column in the *Express Daily News* was terminated on 31 March after she twice defied a managerial decision restraining columnists from writing about the case of Xi Yang (see below). An article critical of Beijing's Hong Kong affairs advisor was also withheld by the paper, as were two pieces about the withdrawal. The paper's editor told Chan she was too troublesome compared with other columnists. (Article 19, Hong Kong Journalists' Association)

Two poets who fled Vietnam in 1989, Nguyen Hong Quang and Nguyen Quoc Binh are in danger of repatriation after the Immigration Department refused their application for political asylum. They face prosecution and probable imprisonment if returned to Vietnam. (PEN)

Two exiled Chinese dissidents were refused visas to Hong Kong to commemorate the fifth anniversary of the student protests in Beijing. Chris Patten reportedly defended the decision to bar journalist Liu Binyan and former Communist official Ruan Ming, both resident in the US, saying Hong Kong did not wish to appear to be challenging China. Chinese authorities said the visit would have been 'provocative'. (*Daily Telegraph*)

Senior journalists expressed fears in early June of a press clampdown under Chinese rule, following a report that Beijing is drawing up regulations to govern the local media. The regulations would reportedly stress 'promoting Chinese interests and the stability of Hong Kong' and would incorporate restrictions to prevent media organisations 'being used as tools to topple the Chinese government'.

Six senior Asian Television (ATV) journalists threatened to resign as a result of a decision by the station to drop part of a documentary on the Tiananmen Square massacre, due to be televised on 4 June. ATV eventually reversed the decision, but acting news controller Poon Fu-yim, assistant news controller Selina Li Yuk-lin, executive editor Lo Wing-hung, managing editor Lui Wan-sang, assignment editor Chui Pui-ying, and city editor Lau Kwok-wah handed in their resignations on 1 June in protest at the attempted self-censorship. (Article 19, Hong Kong Journalists' Association)

Governor Chris Patten decided not to establish an independent Human Rights Commission on 1 June, and also rejected the proposed Equal Opportunities and Access to Information Bills. (*South China Morning Post*)

HUNGARY

On 30 March Laszlo Gyoeri, chairman of the Independent Trade Union of Radio Employees, was suspended from Hungarian Radio. On 7 April Hungarian Radio's main midday news bulletin was cut short owing to industrial action protesting against the management's failure to reverse recent wholesale staff dismissals (*Index* 1&2/1994) and the disciplinary actions taken against union leaders. (SWB)

Under a law passed on 1 April a new committee will investigate whether senior government officials have ever been members of the III/3 secret service department, the post-1956 Special Police militia or the wartime fascist party Arrow Cross. The law has been criticised for opening the way for slanderous accusations and because the relevant government documents are closed for inspection until 2030. (SWB)

On 27 April Hungarian television refused to screen the Green Party's election broadcast because of its alleged anti-Semitic content. (SWB)

The National Election Committee called on the media to observe 'campaign silence' on 3 May, following a complaint by Socialist Party leader Gyula Horn against the programme *Panorama* which had broadcast allegations by a Hungarian émigré that, when he was in prison in 1956, Horn had kicked him in the mouth. Horn also accused the programmes *Newsreel* and *This Week* of carrying slander and lies during the election campaign. (SWB, *Guardian*)

On 14 May former state television chairman Elemer Hankiss (*Index* 3/1993, 1&2/1994), former TV1 controller Gabor Banyai and former TV1 economic director Laszlo Nagy reportedly launched a legal suit against the justice minister, Istvan Balsai, and acting television chairman Gabor Nahlik, accusing them of making false charges and of misappropriation. (SWB)

INDIA

In March Ramesh Singla, youth-wing president of the Congress Party in Punjab, and an Amritsar organisation both reportedly offered substantial rewards for the murder of Sadique Hussain, Pakistani author of the book *Tehrik-e-Mujahideen* (History of Warriors). (*Times of India*)

Pakistani journalist Masood Azhar, director of the monthly magazines *Sadae Mujahid* and *Saute Kashmir*, was arrested in March near the northwestern city of Srinagar, while reporting on the Islamic separatist movement in Kashmir. Reports indicate he has been tortured. (PEN)

Islamic officials in Nagaon issued a *fatwa* against Aminur Rehman, a reporter with the Bengali daily *Samay Prabaha* on 20 March, after he wrote a critical article about a meeting of the Islamic group Viswa Esteema. Two local business people have subsequently offered rewards for his assassination and he has gone into hiding. (PEN)

Ram Narain Gupta, editor of the Varanasi-based daily newspaper *Jaidesh* was shot by unidentified assailants on 9 May. He died the following day. (CPJ)

Recent publication: *Dead Silence — The Legacy of Abuses in Punjab* (Human Rights Watch/Asia & Physicians for Human Rights, May 1994, 103pp)

INDONESIA

Dissident writer Wimanjaya Liotohe is reported to have been interrogated by police on 13 April in connection with his book *Prima Dosa* (Prime Sin) which was banned in January for 'attacking and spreading lies about President Suharto' by reportedly stating that he played a part in the 1965 overthrow of President Sukarno. If convicted for his book, he faces up to seven years and four months in prison. (PEN)

Despite new measures announced in early June aimed at deregulating the media, the information minister has said that the existing ban on foreign investment in the media will remain in force. (International Press Institute)

Recent publication: *The Medan Demonstrations and Beyond* (Human Rights Watch/Asia, May 1994, 14pp)

IRAN

The death is reported of Bishop Haik Housepian Mehr, leader of the Evangelical Council of Pastors in Iran, who disappeared three days after the release of Mehdi Dibaji (*Index* 1&2/1994) which he had worked to secure. Mehr had protested the closure of churches and the torture of converts to Christianity. He was believed to be in the hands of the security forces when he died, but government sources deny they were holding him. (*Times, Independent*, Islamic Republic News Agency)

Writers Ali Akbar Saidi Sirjani and Said Niazi-Kermani were arrested on 14 March and charged with drug trafficking. An intelligence official said on 25 April that the two had confessed to using drugs, making alcoholic drinks, homosexual acts and links with espionage networks and Western counter-revolutionary groups. All these are capital offences. (PEN)

Recent publication: *For Rushdie — Essays by Arab and Muslim Writers in Defense of Free Speech* (George Braziller, New York, 1994, 302pp, $14.95)

IRAQ

Lissy Schmidt, a German reporter for AFP, was shot dead on 3 April near

Suleimaniyah. Kurdish authorities say they have arrested two men who allegedly confessed to being paid by the Iraqi secret police to kill foreigners. Other reports suggest the men were forced to do so after their families were taken hostage. (PEN)

ISRAEL AND OCCUPIED TERRITORIES

A number of journalists have been wounded by Israeli soldiers while reporting in the Occupied Territories: Associated Press photographer John Gaps was shot on 7 March in Gaza; and in the West Bank, Reuter cameraman Mohamed Attallah Hassan was shot on 29 March; Hisham Sharabati of the Worldwide Television News network was shot on 3 April; and cameraman Nidal Hassan was shot on 20 May. (CPJ, RSF, IFJ)

Adnan Abu Hasna, correspondent for *Al-Quds* newspaper and for Al-Qatar Radio, was reportedly arrested at his home in Gaza City on 25 April. It is believed that he is being held under administrative detention. (CPJ)

The Israeli authorities declared the Jericho region a 'closed military zone' on 4 May and barred journalists from entering, following the signing of the autonomy accord between Israel and the PLO. (RSF)

Recent Publications: *Lethal Gunfire and Collective Punishment in the Wake of the Massacre at the Tomb of the*

...ET POURQUOI ON LE JUGERAIT?...
IL N'A RIEN FAIT!

—JiHo

RSF

'Why would we put him on trial?... He hasn't done anything!'

Patriarchs (B'Tselem, March 1994, 17pp); *Discrimination in Education Against The Arab Palestinians in Israel* (Arab Association for Human Rights, April 1994, 23pp); *Summary Execution: Jabalya Refugee Camp, March 28, 1994* (B'Tselem/Palestinian Lawyers for Human Rights, April 1994, 10pp)

ITALY

In early March a law to ensure the purity of the Italian language was reimposed by neo-Fascist councillors in the city of Pavia. (*Times*)

The homes of several dozen members of the computer network Fidonet were raided by police on 10 May in an indiscriminate crackdown against software piracy and appropriation of secret passwords. The raids, which have resulted in the closure of a large part of the network, were reportedly prompted by accusations against two people allegedly involved in distributing illegal copies of computer programmes. (Institute for Global Communications)

JAPAN

Two armed men held newspaper executives hostage at the paper *Asahi Shimbun* for six hours on 1 April in Tokyo to protest at the paper's coverage of the Tokyo tribunal after World War II which, they said, blasphemed the spirits of the dead. The men surrendered after riot police surrounded the building. (FIEJ)

In May, historian Saburo Ienaga finally won a 31-year battle against official attempts to censor schoolbook accounts of the 1937 Rape of Nanking. The Tokyo High Court found that Education Ministry censors had distorted passages about the massacre in a textbook written by Ienaga. Also in May the justice minister, Shigeto Nagano, was forced to resign for saying the Rape of Nanking was a fabrication and that Japan was not an aggressor

in World War II. (*International Herald Tribune*)

JORDAN

Recent publication: *Jordan — Democratization Without Press Freedom* (Article 19, March 1994, 26pp)

KAZAKHSTAN

The country's first multi-party elections were held on 8 March. About a quarter of the legislature's 177 seats were allocated to President Nazarbaev's own nominees, of whom more than half already hold state or government jobs. Members of the independent trade union association, former Communists in the Socialist party, Kazakh nationalists belonging to the Decembrist movement, and members of the newly formed pro-Russian Lad Party, were all barred from standing. Foreign observers said the elections were not free and fair. (*Guardian, Independent*)

Russian journalist Boris Suprunyuk was arrested in Petropavlovsk on 13 April and charged with inciting interethnic discord. Suprunyuk has been active as a spokesman for the Russian community and has reported recently on tensions between Cossack villagers and Kazakh authorities in the Taldy Kurgan region near the Chinese border. (RFE/RL)

KENYA

Four journalists at *The Standard* were arrested following the publication of a report on renewed violence in the Rift Valley. Bureau chief Ngumo wa Kuria and reporter Peter Rianga Makori were arrested on 16 March and charged with subversion for 'an act prejudicial to the security of the state'. It is alleged that the article was 'intended or calculated to promote feelings of hatred or enmity between different races or communities in Kenya'. The paper's managing editor, Kamau Kanyanga, and deputy chief sub-editor, John Nyaosi, were also charged with subversion on 23 March. All four were granted bail on 31 March. Since 1993 only residents, officials and police have been allowed into the Rift Valley area, preventing the reporting or verification of events there. (AI)

Mutegi Njau, news editor of the *Daily Nation* was arrested on 11 April and charged with subversion. The 4 April edition of the paper ran an article which reported an allegation that members of the security forces had attacked a community in the Burnt Forest area of the Rift Valley. Njau is currently free on bail. (Article 19)

The trial began on 12 April of human rights activist and former MP Koigi wa Wamwere (*Index* 10/1993, 1&2/1994) who, along with Charles Kuria Wamwere, James Maigwa and Godfrey Ngengi Njuguna, is charged with attempted robbery with violence. There are concerns that the charges have been fabricated and that the trial is part of a pattern of harassment of those who are trying to investigate incidents in the Rift Valley. (AI)

Bedan Mbugua, editor-in-chief of *The People*, and reporter David Makali were sentenced to five months for contempt on 2 June in connection with an article which claimed that a judicial decision to prevent university professors from organising a union was politically motivated. The paper's lawyer was also imprisoned. (RSF)

Recent publication: *Failing the Democratic Challenge: Freedom of Expression in Multi-Party Kenya 1993* by James J Silk (Robert F Kennedy Memorial Center for Human Rights, February 1994, 76pp)

LEBANON

The information minister banned all private radio and television stations from broadcasting news and other political programmes on 23 March in the wake of the 27 February bombing of a Maronite Christian church in Jounieh. Two newspapers, *Al-Safir* and *Ad-Diyar*, were charged with publishing false news on 26 and 27 March respectively, apparently because of reports on the bombing and the situation of imprisoned suspects. (CCPJ, RSF, Human Rights Watch)

A broadcast of the French television programme *Cercle de Minuit* was halted on 10 June after the information minister telephoned the president of the Lebanese Broadcasting Corporation to order its immediate termination. The programme focuses on Lebanese political and religious issues. A recent government decree bars independent media from broadcasting news or discussing political affairs. (RSF)

MALAWI

Hundreds of publications remained banned during the build-up to the country's first multi-party elections. An exposé of state involvement in the murder of four politicians which appeared in Johannesburg *Weekly Mail* was censored from those editions imported into Malawi. (MISA)

Janet Karim, the editor-in-chief of the *Independent* newspaper, faces a defamation suit following a series of articles alleging corrupt dealings between the managing director of City Motors, Ishmail Sabadia, and members of the government. In April David Nthengwe, the paper's acting editor, reportedly received threats of imprisonment and death from associates of Sabadia. (Article 19)

On 26 April the National Consultative Council voted to ensure that any amendments to fundamental provisions in the new Constitution, including the bill of rights, must be approved by a referendum. The Constitution was passed by Parliament on 16 May. (*International Herald Tribune*)

MALAYSIA

Inter-Press Service correspondent Leah Makabenta was expelled from the country on 3 April because of a report she filed comparing Malaysia's 1969 ethnic riots to the current situation in Bosnia, and for writing a 'very negative article' about the mistreatment of migrant labourers. The expulsion follows the government's bar on all foreign journalists who write negative reports about the country (*Index* 1&2/1994).(PEN)

MAURITANIA

The weekly newspaper *Mauritanie Nouvelles* suspended publication on 22 March after the National Printing House withheld funds which had been donated to the newspaper. (West African Journalists' Association)

On 19 May, the Arabic edition of the magazine *Le Calame* was seized on the order of the director of public freedoms, apparently because it contained extracts from a human rights report issued by Agir Ensemble (Act Together) and the International Federation of Human Rights (FIDH). *Le Calame* has since been suspended for one month. (RSF)

Recent publication: *Mauritania's Campaign of Terror — State-Sponsored Repression of Black Africans* (Human Rights Watch/Africa, April 1994, 156pp)

MEXICO

Three armed men burst into the home of constitutional lawyer and human rights activist Emílio Krieger Vásquez on 26 April and stole the manuscript of his new book on the defence of the Constitution. (Inter-Church Committee for Human Rights)

Two unidentified men tried to enter the Institute of Anthropological Advice for the Maya Region in San Cristóbal de las Casas on 3 May in order, they said, to take away the computer. The Institute has important historical archives which were widely consulted by journalists covering the Chiapas uprising in January. The Institute's coordinator, André Aubry, has received several death threats accusing him of sympathising with the EZLN rebels. (AI)

Jorge Martín Dorantes, editor of the weekly paper *Crucero*, was shot dead on 6 June. He was well known for his controversial reporting of corruption among politicians and local government officials. The motive for his murder is not known. (CPJ)

MONGOLIA

A new law ensuring freedom of expression in the media is reportedly being drafted on the initiative of President Punsalmaagiun Ochirbat. Although the government agency controlling the mass media has been abolished, the media are still not free of political influence. (Presidential Press Service)

MOROCCO

On 17 May three human rights activists were found guilty of threatening state security. Ali Hrach Errass and Ali Aken were sentenced to two years' imprisonment, and Mbarek Tausse to one year, for their part in a peaceful demonstration to campaign for official

recognition of the Berber language. (AI)

NAMIBIA

Two broadcasting executives and a radio presenter from the Namibian Broadcasting Corporation were fined by a tribal court in March after a caller to a live phone-in programme criticised the chief of the Caprivi region. (MISA)

NETHERLANDS

Author Graa Boomsma was found not guilty on 9 June of insulting Dutch war veterans. Eddy Schaaffsma, a journalist with the paper *Nieuwsblad van het Noorden*, who interviewed Boomsma about his novel *The Last Typhoon* in 1992, was also acquitted of the same charge. The novel is based on the experiences of the author's father in the Dutch army in Indonesia in the 1940s. The charges arose over comments Boomsma made in the interview, comparing the Dutch army's conduct to that of the Nazis during World War II. (PEN)

NIGERIA

Between 7 and 9 April three journalists with the magazine *Newsweek* were arrested. Editor-in-chief Dan Agbese, Ray Ekpu, and Yakubu Mohammed were charged with sedition and criminal intent to cause fear, alarm and disaffection among the military and the public following the publication of an interview with a retired Brigadier-General who claimed that General Abacha had no intention of returning the country to democratic rule. The three journalists were granted a presidential pardon on 14 April but are planning a US$700,000 suit against the government over their detention. (CPJ, FIEJ, *Newsweek*, *West Africa*)

Over the weekend of 9 April *Wall Street Journal* reporter Geraldine Brooks was arrested in Port Harcourt where she was reporting a story on unrest in Rivers State relating to the violence in Ogoniland. She was held incommunicado for several days, her notes were confiscated and she was finally deported to the US. (CPJ)

Writer Ken Saro-Wiwa (*Index* 8&9/1993) was arrested on 22 May, along with nine other members of the Movement for the Survival of the Ogoni People, and accused of involvement in the killing of four Ogoni leaders. Saro-Wiwa, who has a heart condition, has been refused medical treatment and has allegedly been tortured. The Nigerian military is reportedly planning to increase its presence in Ogoniland and to set up a tribunal to 'investigate the disturbances in the region'. (PEN)

PAKISTAN

Three Christians charged with blasphemy by leaders of the Islamist party Sepah-e Sahaba were shot outside Lahore High Court on 5 April. Manzoor Masih was shot dead and three others — Rehmat Masih, Salamat Masih and John Joseph — were seriously injured in the attack, which eyewitnesses say was carried out by Sepah-e

Where's Rwanda? It's here.

Sahaba members. Blasphemy is a capital offence under the Penal Code. (AI)

PARAGUAY

Armed police forcibly suppressed a demonstration by farmers in Tacuara on 2 May, killing one and injuring *ABC Color* correspondent Mariano Godoy. (RSF)

PERU

Cecilia Valenzuela and Cesar Hildebrandt (*Index* 5&6/1993) were acquitted of defaming a senior army officer on 20 April, when the Supreme Court unanimously overturned a one-year sentence passed by a lower court in August 1993. (Instituto Prensa y Sociedad)

A Habeas Data suit against Channel 4 journalists Nicolas Lucar and Rosana Cueva (*Index* 1&2/1994) was dismissed in March. The government transferred jurisdiction of the controversial law from

criminal to civil courts on 3 May and Congress is also considering a revision of the law which, many fear, could be used to impose prior restraint. (FIP, Instituto Prensa y Sociedad)

Twelve former *El Diario* journalists accused of terrorism (*Index* 1&2/1994) were acquitted by an anonymous tribunal on 5 April. (FIP)

Antero Gargurevich Oliva, a professor at the Universidad Nacional de Callao who has conducted research into the country's guerrilla and subversion movements, was sentenced to 12 years in prison on 15 April, after being found with subversive documents in his possession. He is reported to be in very poor health. (PEN)

Retired General Luís Cisneros Vizquerra was given a 90-month suspended sentence in May for insulting a superior. The sentence will be enforced if he again expresses ideas considered offensive by the military high command. Legal proceedings are currently under way against three other retired generals — Sinesio Jarama, Germán Parra and José Pastor — for similar offences. (Instituto Prensa y Sociedad)

Luis Velásquez Tagle of the Lima daily *La República* and Channel 13 television was assaulted by police outside his home in Huanunco on 15 May. (Instituto Prensa y Sociedad)

On 18 May Guido Falcon Nivin, Wilfredo Mendoza Flores and Rony Flor Coayla of the weekly *Moquegua al Día* and the radio station Mineria were sentenced to six months in prison for defaming a government official. They had reported a private corruption suit against the official and have been barred from further reporting of the case. (FIP)

In late May Wilfredo Pelaez Guluarte, a journalist for the Chimbote paper *El Diario*, was arrested for non-payment of a fine awarded in a defamation case against the mayor of Chimbote. He had accused the mayor of misappropriation of public funds and nepotism. (Instituto Prensa y Sociedad)

PHILIPPINES

Staff secretary of the Philippine Alliance of Human Rights Advocates, Wilfredo Sibayan, was arrested on 28 March and is believed to be in incommunicado detention at a military camp. Sibayan has been publicly accused by military intelli-

gence of being a leader of the New People's Army. (AI)

A regional court judge issued a temporary restraining order on 27 May, banning a conference on the situation in East Timor which has caused a diplomatic incident with Indonesia. The order was issued four days before the conference was due to begin. The conference eventually went ahead as scheduled, although some delegates were refused permission to attend. (*International Herald Tribune*)

POLAND

Presidential spokesman Andrzej Drzycimski criticised NBC's management of public television as 'careless, tendentious and unprofessional' after the main news programme failed to report Lech Walesa's visit to Estonia on 10 May. The editor responsible was suspended. (RFE/RL)

Recent publication: *Human Rights and Democratization in Poland* (Commission on Security and Cooperation in Europe, January 1994, 16pp)

ROMANIA

Amendments to the criminal code proposed in March would make defamation of the country or nation and communication of false news with intent to impair the state or its foreign relations punishable by up to five years in prison. The amendments are due to be reviewed by the Chamber of Deputies.(AI, SWB)

On 21 March the Bucharest

Supreme Court barred its officials from giving information to journalists by telephone, following the example of several other government departments including the intelligence service and the health and agriculture ministries. Officials are becoming increasingly reluctant to supply journalists with routine information without official permission. (Reuter)

Recent Publication: *Romania: Criminal Law on the Wrong Track* (Amnesty International, March 1994, 9pp)

RUSSIA

Andrei Azderdzis, State Duma deputy and publisher of the weekly *Who's Who*, was shot dead outside his Moscow home on 26 April. The paper had recently published a list of 226 alleged mafia godfathers. (PEN)

On 3 May, World Press Freedom Day, the Russian government and parliament were reported to be preparing a draft law on the control of state news broadcasts which would dictate the type of information broadcast by state television and radio and which would forbid 'comment and analysis'. (Reuter, RFE/RL)

RWANDA

Reporters Sans Frontières has called on the UN Human Rights Commission to demand that the Rwandan authorities close the station Radio-Television Libre des Milles Collines (RTLM). Since 6 April, when the presi-

RSF has checked out the South Korean press for you... It's a bit like the Chinese press...Even so, it's not bad...

dents of Rwanda and Burundi were killed, the station has consistently stirred up hatred and incited violence between the Hutu majority and Tutsi minority, according to RSF. In anticipation of the formation of an international commission to investigate gross human rights violations in Rwanda, RSF also demanded that all of RTLM's journalists and promoters should be tried. (RSF)

Abbot André Sibomana, publisher of the independent magazine *Kinyamateka* and head of the Rwandan Journalists' Association, was detained by pro-government militia in Butare in early June. (RSF)

SAO TOMÉ & PRINCIPE

On 13 May Carlos Borboletas, chief editor of the government periodical *Noticias*, and Telmo Trindade, a producer at national radio, were given a six-month suspended sentence for 'abuse of press freedom' and ordered to pay US$1,000 in damages to President Miguel Trovoada, who had sued them for defamation over their alle-

gations that he had withheld some 60 decrees prepared by the government and submitted to him for signature. (*West Africa*)

SAUDI ARABIA

Abd Ar-Rahman Al-Ashmawi, poet and professor of Arabic at Al-Imam University, was arrested on 13 April. His poetry is said to be critical of the government. He was released without charge on 11 May. Writer and businessman Nasir Abdulkarim was also arrested on 27 April, possibly in connection with the arrest of Al-Ashmawi. He was released on 19 May. (PEN)

SENEGAL

Several journalists have apparently suffered professionally for their trade union activity following the creation of the Independent Union of Journalists (SAJES). Union leaders Cheikh Tidiane Fall, Dijb Diedhiou, Jacques Diouf, Abdallah Faye and Ibrahima Diouf were all demoted on 17 May. (West African Journalists' Association)

The Paris-based weekly *Jeune Afrique* was banned from sale for one year on 2 June and its director-general Bechir Ben Yahmed given a six-month suspended sentence for defamation. (RSF)

SERBIA-MONTENEGRO

Forty-two ethnic Albanian families were evicted from their flats in Kosovo in the first quarter of this year and in each case the evicting authorities

gave no reason for their action. The flats were re-allocated to Serbian families. (Council for the Protection of Human Rights and Liberties)

Shaip Beqiri, writer and director of the Albanian-language magazine *Forumi*, was arrested on 19 March and summarily sentenced to 60 days in prison. The arrest followed a tussle between his son and the son of the Serbian rector of Prishtina University, in which Beqiri intervened. (PEN)

The news staff of the Serbian newspaper *Knjizevna Rec* were dismissed during April. The stated reasons for the dismissals were lack of patriotism, misuse of the paper's space, and publishing the works of 'certain enemies of Serbian national interest' such as Allen Ginsberg and Hans Magnus Enzensberger. (Radio B92)

Over a dozen foreign correspondents have been barred from working in the Yugoslav Federation, following the withdrawal of their press accreditation on 13 April. (PEN)

On 19 May the government withdrew widely criticised legal proposals that would have ended the right of independent media in Serbia to receive assistance from abroad. (*International Herald Tribune*)

Recent publications: *Police Violence Against Ethnic Albanians in Kosovo Province* (Amnesty International, April 1994, 15pp); *Human Rights Abuses of Non-Serbs in Kosovo, Sandzak and Vojvodina*

(Human Rights Watch/Helsinki, May 1994, 11pp)

The government said it would allow the *Far Eastern Economic Review* to circulate 2,000 copies per week from May, after severely restricting its sales over the last seven years. The magazine's circulation was cut to 500 copies in 1987, because of alleged interference in domestic policies. (*International Herald Tribune*)

Patrick Daniel, the editor of *Business Times*, its technology editor Kenneth James, the Monetary Authority director Tharman Shanmugaratnam, and Crosby Securities economists Many Bhaskaran and Raymond Foo (*Index* 1&2/1994), were found guilty of leaking classified economic information on 31 March. They were fined a total of US$20,000. (*Guardian*)

Ilaria Alpi of Italian TV station RAI-3, and Miran Hrovatin, a Slovene camera operator based in Italy, were shot dead outside the Italian embassy in Mogadishu on 20 March. Local residents suggested that the shootings related to a labour dispute, but a UN military spokesman said that the motive was robbery. (News wires)

The names of 36 residents of the town of Eshowe in Gezinsila township have appeared on a hit list found on 30 March. The names include ANC officials and members, as well as activists in women's, peace and development projects and in the Local Government Negotiations Forum. Chief BI Zulu of the Inkatha Freedom Party has reportedly been implicated in the threats against Eshowe residents. (AI)

It was reported in April that the South African Publications Act is to be amended, so that books and other publications will no longer be banned for bringing any section of the population into ridicule or contempt; for harming the relations between any sections of the population; or for being prejudicial to the safety of the State. (South African Library)

The *Star*'s chief photo-journalist, Ken Oosterbroek, was shot dead while covering a gun battle between hostel dwellers and the National Peace Keeping Force (NPKF) on 18 April. He was hit at close-range by a dum-dum bullet, apparently fired by the NPKF. (IFJ)

Several journalists covering a rally held by the Afrikaaner Resistance Movement (AWB) on 27 April were badly beaten by AWB members. Michael Allan of the *New York Daily News*, Namibian photo-journalist Sylvia Moresche and *Times* photographer Adrian Brooks were among the reporters invited to the rally by AWB leader Eugene Terreblanche. (*Times*, *Daily Telegraph*)

On 9 June Joe Modise, defence minister in the new government, sought a legal injunction to prevent the *Weekly Mail and Guardian* from publishing a story about the attempt of 23 former members of the South African Defence Force's Directorate of Covert Collection to secure an amnesty for past abuses. The ANC issued a statement condemning the injunction, which Modise withdrew on 14 June. (MISA)

Recent publication: *Impunity for Human rights Abuses in Two Homelands — Reports on KwaZulu and Bophuthatswana* (Human Rights Watch/Africa, March 1994, 23pp)

Three publishers were arrested in March and accused of having published pro-North Korean material. Lee Song-woo and Kim Byong-hak, owner and managing director respectively of Ilbit Publishing Company, were arrested on 19 March; and Kim Yon-in, owner of the Heem Publishing Company, was arrested on 23 March and released the same day. Park Chi-kwan, chief editor of the Il-t'eo Publishing Company was also arrested on 19 April and is being held for interrogation about the North Korean novel *The Smelters*, 200 copies of which were seized shortly after his arrest. It is believed he may be charged for publishing 'anti-state' material, although the book was apparently openly available in bookshops. (PEN)

Three more members of the Heemangsae (Bird of Hope)

singing troupe (*Index 1&2/1994*) were arrested under the National Security Law on 15 April. Ho Myong-soon, Ahn Song-hae and Choi Kyong-ah were arrested by police who also confiscated books and music tapes. Like the five arrested earlier, they are accused of planning a musical based on the pro-North Korea book *Shining Path* and for distributing information about the musical on a computer network. (AI)

SRI LANKA

Hemal Warnakula, head of Sinhalese programming for Radio Veritas, received several anonymous death threats in March, after he had reported a request from RSF that the investigation into the 1990 murder of human rights activist Richard De Zoysa be reopened. (RSF)

The well-known Tamil exile Sabarotnam Sabalingham was shot dead in Paris on 1 May by two Tamil youths. He had been working on a history of the Tamil militant movements which exposed assassinations among rival groups. (*Sri Lanka Monitor*)

SUDAN

About 30 people were arrested in Khartoum on 10 March after attending a meeting to commemorate the execution of 28 army officers in 1990. The anniversary of the executions has become a rallying point for opposition to the military government. Most were released after signing an undertaking not to campaign against the

government, or to leave Khartoum without prior permission. (AI)

The daily *Al Sudani al-Doulia* was closed by order of the president on 4 April for 'trying to destroy the National Salvation Revolution and its symbols'. Owner and chief editor Mahjoub Mohammed al-Hassan Erwa and two journalists, Ahmad Ali Bagadi and Mutwakil Abdel Daffeh, were arrested for spreading false news. Bagadi and Daffeh were released around 18 April. The paper has carried reports on alleged government corruption and has called for greater press freedom. (PEN)

SWEDEN

Serbian journalist Sevdail Zejnullahu was reported to be facing deportation on 13 June. Zejnullahu, who worked for the paper *Bota Re* in Kosovo, fled to Sweden after Serbian authorities closed the paper in 1992. (IFJ)

TAJIKISTAN

Olim Abdulov, a journalist with the Tajik state television network, was reported murdered near Dushanbe on 16 May. Two days later Khoshvakht Haydarsho, a reporter for the pro-government daily paper *Jumhuriyat*, was found dead in front of his home. Judicial enquiries have been opened into the killings, which observers believe were politically motivated. Abdulov was well known as a critic of the Communist government; and Haydarsho has recently written articles on organised

crime and political corruption. (RSF)

TANZANIA

Pascal Shija, editor of the bi-weekly *The Express*, was arrested on 11 March, after the publication of an article headed 'Is Tanzania a big garbage dump?' He has reportedly been charged with publishing 'seditious words with the intent to bring hatred or excite disaffection against the state' and released on bail. An application for *The Express* to publish daily has been turned down. (International Press Institute, PEN)

TOGO

Martin Dossou Gbenouga, the managing editor of the opposition bi-weekly *La Tribune des Democrates*, was sentenced on 6 May to five years' imprisonment for defaming the president. The charges arose from an article which said that President Eyadema had subjugated the country to France and called for him to be tried for high treason. (*West Africa*, RSF)

TUNISIA

Foreign media and journalists were censored by government authorities during the run-up to the national elections on 20 March. The French daily *Le Monde* was banned and its special correspondent Jacques de Barrin declared *persona non grata*. A television crew from the French network France 2 was refused entry to the country on 18 March. The 23 March issue of *Libération*, which carried an article on Tunisian democracy, was seized. The French monthly *Le Monde Diplomatique*, the British daily *The Guardian* and the Moroccan weekly *Les Nouvelles du Nord* were also temporarily banned. (RSF, IFJ)

Moncef Marzouki, a human rights activist and medical school professor, was arrested on 24 March and charged with 'spreading false information liable to disturb public order and insulting the judiciary authorities'. The charges apparently arise from an interview that he gave to a Spanish newspaper. (AI, American Association for the Advancement of Science)

Mohammed Hedi Sassi was sentenced to four years' imprisonment on 19 May on account of his political activities with the Tunisian Workers' Communist Party (PCOT) and distribution of leaflets condemning restrictions to freedom of expression. He is believed to have been tortured while in detention in Tunis. (AI)

TURKEY

Writer Mehmet Bayrak was sentenced to two years in prison and fined on 8 March on account of the book *Kurt Halk Turkuleri* (Kurdish Folk Songs) which he was editing. (PEN)

Nazim Babaoglu, a reporter for *Özgür Gündem*, reportedly disappeared on 12 March in the town of Slverek. The security forces deny any knowledge of his whereabouts. (PEN)

Three crew members from German Flash TV — Peter Wymar, Michael Enger and Corinna Gutstadt — were attacked by police in Tatvan on 19 March. On 23 March they were detained and kept blindfolded by police while trying to report on a local election campaign. On 16 March Tacettin Vural of Ankara Flash TV was among five journalists beaten by police at Antalya Airport while covering the prime minister's election campaign. (PEN)

The press Turkish style

Zana Sezen, editor-in-chief of *Azadi*, was sentenced to just under two years in prison on 25 March for articles published in *Azadi* in October 1993. (PEN)

Huseyin Tekin, news manager of the paper *Emegin Bayragi*, was arrested on 8 April and accused of disseminating separatist propaganda and insulting security officers. (PEN)

Derya Tanrivermis and Zafer Sakin were detained after the Anti-Terror Branch of Ankara Police Headquarters raided the offices of the magazine *Alinteri* (Toil) on 17 April. They were

released on 6 May. (RSF, PEN)

On 3 May Bulent Aydin, chief editor of *Yeni Ulke*, was sentenced to five months in prison and fined for 'making propaganda for the PKK'. (PEN)

Aysenur Zarakolu, director of the Belge Publishing House, was committed to prison on 4 May, after a five month sentence for 'advocating separatism' was ratified. She is believed to be the first publisher to be sentenced under article 8 of the Anti-Terror Law and there are fears that her imprisonment could set a precedent for the incarceration of other publishers. The charges arose from her publication of Ismail Besikci's book *CHP Programme-1931, Kurdish Problem* (*Index* 7/1993, 1&2/1994). Besikci still has many cases pending against him, all for his writing. His prison sentences currently amount to more than 30 years. (PEN)

Serif Avsar, brother of the European *Özgür Gündem* representative was found dead on 7 May, two weeks after he disappeared. He had been shot in the head twice. Eyewitnesses reported seeing two men abducting him on 22 April. (AI)

Recent publications: *Silence is Killing Them — Annual Report on the Situation of Human Rights in Northern Kurdistan and the Kurds of Turkey* (International Association for Human Rights in Kurdistan, 1994, 64pp); *A Matter of Power*

— *State Control of Women's Virginity in Turkey* (Human Rights Watch Women's Rights Project, June 1994, 38pp)

UKRAINE

As of the 24 May it is reported that Russian journalists working in the Ukraine are being denied official accreditation after being accused of 'rabid and dishonest' reporting of events in the Crimean region. At present it is believed that only one Russian journalist, Vladimir Lyaskala, has received accreditation. (CPJ)

USA

Freedom Forum reports that 36 per cent of the 384 government-supported colleges and universities they surveyed have rules against hate speech, though such restrictions are probably unconstitutional. Further, about 47 per cent of the institutions bar 'indecent' language, which is protected by the First Amendment, and 28 per cent prohibit advocacy of offensive points of view (*Index* 7/1992, p6). (*Editor and Publisher*)

In March, the publisher Holt, Reinhart and Winston refused to make some 300 changes to a health textbook ordered by the Texas Board of Education and withdrew the book from Texas schools. The Board was responding to pressure from the religious right. (Reuter)

Daniel Buron, a Haitian political activist living in Miami, was shot dead on 9 March. Buron and two other opponents of the Haitian military dictatorship, were attacked after attending a meeting of the anti-military organization Veye Yo. (AP, *New York Times*)

On 11 March, after a national protest, the California Board of Education restored three stories by Alice Walker and Annie Dillard to the list of selections for a statewide English test (*Index* 1&2/1994). (*Newsletter on Intellectual Freedom*)

On 29 March the *Cincinnati Herald*, an African-American newspaper, was firebombed after publishing an article about Arab Muslims. No one was injured, but the newsroom was destroyed. (AP)

In early April, a federal judge barred the government from discharging six gay service members until their lawsuit challenging the new 'don't ask, don't tell' policy on homosexuals in the military is resolved. The suit charges that the policy violates their rights of free speech and equal protection. The legality of the policy was weakened on 2 June, when a federal judge ordered that army nurse Col Margarethe Cammermeyer, the highest-ranking officer to challenge the previous military policy on gays, be reinstated (*Index* 5&6/1993, 8&9/1993). (National press)

On 7 April David LaMacchia, a Massachusetts Institute of Technology student, was charged with defrauding computer software producers by setting up a computer bulletin board system (BBS) through which copyrighted software could be copied for free. LaMacchia's lawyer argues that a BBS operator should be given the same First Amendment protection as a newspaper editor (*Index* 7/1991). (*Boston Globe*)

A Washington, DC Circuit Court reversed its earlier ruling on 3 May and denied writer Dan Moldea the opportunity to argue his charge of libel in court. Moldea wanted to sue the *New York Times Book Review* over a 1989 review of his book, *Interference: How Organized Crime Influences Professional Football*, in which the reviewer accused Moldea of 'too much sloppy journalism'. The case was seen as a test of whether opinions stated in reviews are protected by the First Amendment. The Circuit Court ruled in February that the sloppiness accusation could be evaluated by a jury as a statement of fact and a determination of libel was possible but, in response to a petition by the *Times*, the same panel of judges reconsidered their decision and, in a highly unusual reversal, upheld the 1992 ruling of a lower court that the review was 'substantially true' and therefore protected. (*The Nation, Columbia Journalism Review*)

President Clinton signed the Freedom of Access to Clinic Entrances Act on 26 May, making it a crime to prevent women from entering abortion clinics. Claiming an infringement of their freedom of speech, assembly and religion, the American Life League immediately filed suit to block enforcement of the law. The month before, the Supreme Court heard arguments on the constitutionality of a ruling which limited anti-abortion speech by Operation Rescue outside a clinic in Florida. That ruling is more restrictive than the new law. (*Boston Globe*)

In a case involving an anti-abortion group in Kentucky, the Supreme Court upheld a ruling on 1 June that 'inappropriate' groups may be barred from government-sponsored public events such as fairs. The Court also upheld a ban on the posting of the Ten Commandments in a Georgia courthouse and ruled, in an Illinois case, that public employees can be dismissed for making insubordinate statements, even if some of the statements are protected speech. (AP)

Recent publications: *Sex & Sensibility: Reflections on Forbidden Mirrors and the Will to Censor* (Marcia Pally, Ecco Press, 1994, 198pp); *Artistic Freedom Under Attack II* (People for the American Way, 1994); *The News That Didn't Make the News and Why* (Carl Jensen, Four Walls Eight Windows, 1993, 248pp)

UZBEKISTAN

Uzbek writer Mamadali Makhmudov was arrested on 3 March and charged with possessing firearms. It is thought that the charge was fabricated as part of a crackdown against the banned opposition Erk party, although Makhmudov is not known to be a member of the party. (AI)

Poet Vasilya Inayatova was arrested by Uzbek police in Kazakhstan on 12 May and forcibly returned to Uzbekistan, where she was held for four days. She had been travelling to a human rights conference in Alma Ata. (PEN)

VENEZUELA

The discovery in April of a secret mass grave in the remote state of Zulia has prompted concerns that the army is killing local indigenous peasants in disputes over land tenure. The grave contains dozens of bodies bearing signs of close-range gunshot wounds to the head, many of which appear to have been buried recently. (AI)

ZAIRE

Sylvie Lumu-Nseya was detained on 15 March for two days after her husband, Kalala Mbenga-Kalao of the opposition paper *La Tempête des Tropiques*, went abroad to receive a free speech award. (PEN)

A unit of the civil guard seized the 16 April edition of the opposition newspaper *Le Phare* and burned it. News vendors selling the paper have been harassed and some were detained following the publication of an article on the resignation of the vice president of the High Council of the Republic. (AI)

ZAMBIA

On 8 April police questioned Bright Mwape of *The Post* (*Index* 1&2/1994) and theatened to charge him after he quoted a former minister as saying that President Chiluba was 'a twit'. Section 69 of the Penal code makes it an offence intentionally to publish or broadcast insults against the president. (MISA)

Compiled by: Laura Bruni, Gary Campbell, Juliet Dryden, Anna Feldman, Jason Garner, Oren Gruenbaum, Robin Jones, Annie Knibb, Nan Levinson, George McDonald, Robert Maharajh, Philippa Nugent, Natasha Pairaudeau, and Han Shih Toh.

CONTRIBUTORS

ANNA J ALLOTT is senior research fellow in Burmese studies at the School of Oriental and African Studies, London University.

NOAM CHOMSKY is a Professor in the department of Linguistics and Philosophy at the Massachussetts Institute of Technology in Cambridge, Mass. Radical politician, media guru, America's foremost dissident and, according to his latest biographers in *Manufacturing Consent: Noam Chomsky and the Media*, commentator on professional football, he is also a prolific writer. He has published widely on linguistics, philosophy, intellectual history, contemporary issues, international affairs and human rights.

PETER ELAM is a specialist on Hungarian affairs, at St Antony's College, Oxford, UK.

PENELOPE FARMER is a novelist. Her most recent publication is *Snakes and Ladders* (Littlebrown/Abacus, London, 1993).

NADINE GORDIMER was educated in South Africa and now lives in Johannesburg. In 1991 she was awarded the Nobel Prize for Literature. Her books include *The Conservationist*, *Burger's Daughter*, *July's People*, *A Sport of Nature* and *My Son's Story*. Among her collections of short stories are *A Soldier's Embrace*,

Something Out There, *Selected Stories* and *Jump*. Her new novel, *None to Accompany Me*, will be published this year (Bloomsbury, London).

VÁCLAV HAVEL, the world-renowned playwright, was a prominent member of the Czech cultural underground in the 1960s, with the literary magazine *Tvar* and the independent Theatre on the Balustrade. He founded the Charter 77 human rights movement and spent four years in prison for subversion. After the Velvet Revolution, he became president of Czechoslovakia, subsequently the Czech Republic.

GENEVIEVE HESSE is a journalist with Reporters Sans Frontières.

SHERE HITE's reports on human sexuality have sold worldwide. Her most recent works include *The Hite Report on the Family* (Bloomsbury, London, 1994) and a first novel, *The Divine Comedy of Ariadne and Jupiter* (Peter Owen, London, 1994).

SHADA ISLAM is a correspondent in Brussels for the *Far Eastern Economic Review*.

DONALD KENRICK has worked for Gypsy civil rights for many years. He is the author of *Destiny of Europe's Gypsies, a study of the Nazi period*.

GARA LAMARCHE is associate

director of Human Rights Watch and director of its Free Expression Project.

ISABEL LIGNER is a French journalist working in the UK with the Alternative Information Network (AIM).

DAVID MILLER is a research fellow with the Glasgow University Media Group. He is the author of *Don't Mention the War: Northern Ireland, Propaganda and the Media,* to be published this year by Pluto Press, London.

MILICA PESIC represents the Alternative Information Network (AIM) in London, UK.

DAVID PETRASEK is on sabbatical leave from his post as coordinator of refugee work at the International Secretariat of Amnesty International. The views expressed in the article are the author's own.

MILEN RADEV is a Bulgarian cartoonist, illustrator and graphic designer working in Berlin. He regularly reports for the BBC World Service on East German issues.

MARTIN SMITH is author of *Burma: Insurgency and the Politics of Ethnicity* (Zed Books, London, 1991 and 1993), and *State of Fear: Censorship in Burma* (Article 19, London, 1991).

JON SNOW, prominent broadcaster and news presenter, covered the South African elections for UK Independent Television News.

BOB SUTCLIFFE teaches international economics and development in the University of the Basque Country, Bilbao.

LESZEK SZARUGA is a poet, critic and former editor of the underground literary journal *Puls*.

BECHIR ZNAGIE is a journalist with *Libération* in Morocco.

Index wishes to acknowledge the contribution from the European Commission for the translations from *La Lettre* of Reporters Sans Frontières.

Back Issues

Most back issues of *Index on Censorship* are available from:
Dawsons Back Issues,
Cannon House,
Folkestone,
Kent CT19 5EE, UK
Fax 0303 850440
Volumes 1-14 £24 per volume;
Volumes 15-22 £30 per volume.

DAVID HOLDEN 1959 — 1994

NIGEL PARRY

David Holden, writer and broadcaster, died from a brain tumour on 20 April, aged 34.

DAVID Holden was one of the most promising writers of his generation, who in his fiction and journalism was developing a unique mid-Atlantic voice marked by its humour, compassion and enquiring scepticism. Before graduating from Dartmouth College in 1981, he spent a year as an exchange student at University College London, an experience which marked the beginning of his love affair with this country, and particularly London, where he eventually settled.

His fascination with the connections between Britain and America is one of the main themes in his collection of short stories *This is What Happens When You Don't Pay Attention,* published in 1991.

Index was the focus of his journalism in the last years of his life. His ability to capture the imagination with humour and verbal precision made him a formidable champion of the cause of free speech, not least in the many schools he visited to give speeches on censorship. It was typical of his courage and conviction that only weeks before his death, he was in Amsterdam for 'Guardians of Dissent', the annual free-speech conference organised by *Index's* Dutch Committee.

His passion for nature and the environment led him to move into broadcasting in 1993, where he soon began to stamp his distinctively witty style upon radio programmes such as *Costing The Earth, The Natural History Programme* and *The Food Programme.* David once described himself in a *Times* author profile as an 'utter man of mystery'. To his many friends, however, he was an enchanting presence who shared his life with them generously and candidly.   *Matthew d'Ancona*

WHEN David left *Index* in January 1993 for Papua New Guinea we were sorry to see him leave, but his enthusiasm for the adventure was infectious and undeniable. He kept in touch, not just by postcard, but more powerfully by the series of tape recordings he had made for the BBC. His reports were witty, informative and moving. The description of a leatherback turtle struggling to shore at night to lay and bury her eggs (an event requiring his sprinting trouserless along a beach through a profound darkness illuminated only by lightning and his own commentary) was as immediate and personal as that medium allows.

Despite his illness he was determined to live while he remained alive. If he was to be ill, then illness would have to take a number and wait its turn. For a time, too short a time, it did.

Walking with David was like accompanying a force of nature. Candy wrappers and leaves were swept up at his approach and left swirling in his wake. So it was with his images and ideas. In midwestern America there are two forms of tornado alert. A tornado watch indicates merely that weather conditions are right; a tornado warning declares that one has actually been spotted. While the leaves on earth now lie where they fall, there is a David Holden warning in heaven, and the angels have been grounded.

Josh Passell

DAVID Holden was the one who kept the Dutch Committee of *Index* alive and active. By exaggerating the value of our work, by serving pints of beer after long days, and above all by proving that the fight for freedom of expression does not have to be so grave as the crime of censorship itself. No one else could have captured the necessity of *Index* in slogans like: 'If Samuel Beckett had been born in Czechoslovakia we'd still be waiting for Godot.' He had it printed on a t-shirt. Even though all of them — Czechoslovakia, Beckett and David himself — have ceased to exist, I will continue to wear the t-shirt, because it fits me well. It will remind me not to let gravity get the best of me.

David was extremely sensitive to all that is wrong in the world, and at the same time completely unable to accept its existence, a contrast which is reflected in his writing; beautiful prose, stylish and witty. But at its heart, a darkness for which melancholy is far too mild a word. He couldn't live with the reality that no matter how many walls had fallen and dictators scattered, censorship is still a deafening force.

Chris Keulemans

Over 200 guests celebrated the relaunch of *Index* at a dinner sponsored by *Esquire* magazine in London on 3 May, World Press Freedom Day. Jon Snow was Master of Ceremonies. Above, some of the speakers. From left to right: Stephen Spender, Salman Rushdie, Ursula Owen (Editor), Juliet Stephenson and Michael Grade.

Forthcoming:

CHRISTOPHER HIRD, TED TURNER, CLIVE HOLLICK on media ownership
JULIAN BARNES, A S BYATT, JOHN BERGER and others: Sarajevo 2001
SPECIAL REPORT: RADIO IN AFRICA by Adewale Maja-Pearce
COUNTRY FILES: Britain, Turkey, Poland, Cuba, Hong Kong
NEW WRITING FROM LATIN AMERICA by Andrew Graham-Yooll
THE FAMILY, LANGUAGE & NATIONALISM: Michael Ignatieff, Ranko Bugarski
ABDULLAHI AN-NA'IM on human rights in Islam

Also: the media and elections in Brazil, gay writing, fatwas in Bangladesh